FIGHTING
— FOR —
G.O.D.
(GOLD, OIL, AND DRUGS)

Jeremy Begin & Lauren Salk

Fighting for G.O.D. (Gold, Oil & Drugs)

Published by:
TrineDay
PO Box 577
Walterville, OR 97489
1-800-556-2012
www.TrineDay.com
publisher@TrineDay.com

Begin, Jeremy and Lauren Salk
    Fighting for G.O.D.— 1st ed.
    p. cm.   (acid-free paper)
    (ISBN-13) 978-0-9777953-3-8 (ISBN-10) 0-9777953-3-0
    1. Political corruption—United States. 1. Title

First Edition
10 9 8 7 6 5 4 3 2 1

Printed in the USA
Distribution to the trade by:
    Independent Publishers Group (IPG)
    814 North Franklin Street
    Chicago, Illinois 60610
    312.337.0747
    www.ipgbook.com

Publisher's Caveat

Looking behind the curtains of our everyday world-view, trying to understand how the world really works, one is confronted with a reality of duplicity and confusion, and outrageous scenarios that shred our "official" history leaving one searching through questionable claims of conspiracy, coincidence and complacency. Researching secret history is fraught with danger, for around suspicious events with their accompanying suspect "official" stories there always swirl both misinformation and disinformation that a person must ponder. "Cliffs of belief" arise, tempting one to leap into pools of ignorance, prejudice and contrived dialectic. There have been several false memes introduced into the 9/11 truth movement to disarray, divide and befuddle researchers. And also to provide outlandish claims, which can then be used to deflect critiques of the "official" line. So please be aware — do not be afraid to read anything — but do not believe everything you read or see ... anywhere. *Caveat lector!*

Peace,
Kris Millegan
Publisher
TrineDay

FIGHTING FOR G.O.D.
(GOLD, OIL & DRUGS)

"THE ILLEGAL WE DO IMMEDIATELY. THE UNCONSTITUTIONAL TAKES A LITTLE LONGER."

—HENRY KISSINGER
NEW YORK TIMES, OCT. 28, 1973

Dedicated to those who died that day.

CHAPTER ONE

THE DAY THAT CHANGED EVERYTHING...

THE TRAGIC EVENTS OF SEPTEMBER 11, 2001 WILL FOREVER BE IMPRINTED IN THE MINDS OF THOSE WHO WITNESSED THEM THAT DAY IN PERSON OR ON THEIR TELEVISIONS. FEW OF US WILL EVER BE ABLE TO UNDERSTAND THE PAIN AND GRIEF FELT BY THOSE WHO LOST FAMILY MEMBERS OR FRIENDS DURING THE CATASTROPHE.

And yet, U.S. troops were already dying for God and Country by the time the official 9/11 Commission Report came out. After massive Administration stonewalling, it explained to us just how our incredible intelligence apparatus and air defense system had been thwarted by some cave-dwelling Arabs armed with box cutters. Most Americans celebrated this report, satisfied that they finally knew the truth, and assured that steps were being taken so that something like this would never happen again.

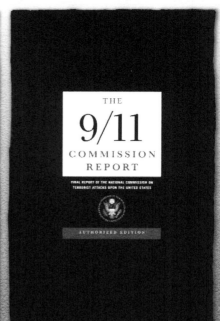

ONLY 9/11 TRUTH WILL SET US FREE!

But there were some, including family members of 9/11 victims, who didn't find the Commission's report altogether satisfying. The Commission's investigation had started with an assumption: that a massive intelligence lapse had failed to prevent an attack which was the sole responsibility of Muslim Fundamentalists led by Osama bin Laden. The Commission never considered the possibility that this assumption might be wrong. And when contradictory evidence was presented, that evidence was simply ignored.

By now, the amount of evidence that has come to light contradicting the official story is so overwhelming that it has prompted a world-wide movement of people who believe that another explanation exists for the events of 9/11. Although the evidence was scarcely discussed in the mainstream media for years, there are now hundreds of millions of people who believe that the true masterminds were perhaps two dozen people in the U.S. Government itself, in collusion with a few top Pakistani, Israeli, and British officials. This cabal was directly complicit in the attacks which have been used to justify repressive legislation and...

"... a war that will not end in our lifetimes."

CHENEY

FIGHTING FOR G.O.D. (Gold, Oil & Drugs)

To understand the truth of 9/11, it is not enough merely to examine the numerous anomalies which contradict official accounts of what happened on and around the day of the attacks. Although we will do this, we should first examine historical groups and patterns that have existed over the past several centuries. Otherwise, we will never understand why a powerful elite would have masterminded such a plan, which is much more important than figuring out how they might have done it.

George W. Bush · Dick Cheney · Bill Clinton · George H.W. Bush · Rockefeller · JP Morgan

There is a saying in certain circles that "GOD equals Gold plus Oil plus Drugs." Those who control these three things have the greatest power over major events on this planet. It is clear that those who stood to gain, and who would have had the ability to orchestrate 9/11, include key figures in Wall Street and International Finance, Oil Barons, and Drug Lords. The wars that were fought, and are being fought for them, are controlled by the Military-Industrial-Intelligence Complex of the United States.

A common player in all of this is the secret society Skull & Bones. While not the "master organization" itself, we shall see that this society has served as a critical conduit for an elite network to put the right people in the right places.

Neocon pundits decry this sort of statement as a conspiracy theory, evidently oblivious to the fact that the official explanation of 9/11 is also a conspiracy theory. This theory blames Muslim conspirators. Another blames a criminal cabal within our own government. President Woodrow Wilson was himself aware of such a cabal and lamented the unwitting aid he had given it.

"We have come to be one of the worst ruled, one of the most completely controlled governments in the civilized world — no longer a government of free opinion, no longer a government by... a vote of the majority, but a government by the opinion and duress of a small group of dominant men. Some of the biggest men in the United States, in the field of commerce and manufacture, are afraid of something. They know that there is a power somewhere so organized, so subtle, so watchful, so interlocked, so complete, so pervasive, that they had better not speak above their breath when they speak in condemnation of it."

WILSON

WE'LL START BY EXAMINING AN OFTEN OVERLOOKED ASPECT OF THE ELITES' CONTROL GRID, THE MONEY SYSTEM. MORE PEOPLE ARE BECOMING AWARE OF JUST HOW MUCH POWER TRANSNATIONAL CORPORATIONS HAVE OVER THE ECONOMY AND POLITICS. BUT, BECAUSE THE DISCUSSION IS CLOAKED IN COMPLEX-SOUNDING ECONOMICS JARGON, FEW PEOPLE, EVEN AMONG ACTIVISTS, UNDERSTAND THE MONEY SYSTEM ITSELF.

THE MONEY CURRENTLY USED IN THE UNITED STATES IS REGULATED BY THE DECEPTIVELY NAMED FEDERAL RESERVE SYSTEM. IN REALITY, THIS INSTITUTION IS NOT FEDERAL, BUT A PRIVATE, FOR-PROFIT ORGANIZATION. THE GOVERNMENT HAS THE CONSTITUTIONAL AUTHORITY TO ISSUE CURRENCY, BUT IT HAS GIVEN THIS RIGHT AWAY. NOW, WHEN THE GOVERNMENT NEEDS MONEY, IT BORROWS IT FROM THE FEDERAL RESERVE, THEN HAS TO PAY IT BACK WITH INTEREST. THIS INTEREST IS WHERE MUCH OF YOUR UNCONSTITUTIONAL FEDERAL INCOME TAX GOES, WHICH IS WHAT MOST PEOPLE FAIL TO COMPREHEND. INFRASTRUCTURE IS PAID FOR BY OTHER TAXES. SCHOOLS ARE FUNDED BY LOCAL STATE AND PROPERTY TAXES, HIGHWAYS ARE PAID FOR BY TOLLS AND TAXES ON GAS. THE FEDERAL INCOME TAX IS A SCAM TO TAKE OUR WEALTH AND PUT IT INTO BANKERS' POCKETS. THE FEDERAL RESERVE WIELDS TREMENDOUS POWER OVER THE U.S. ECONOMY, INCLUDING THE POWER TO CONTROL THE AMOUNT OF CURRENCY IN CIRCULATION. JUST HOW IMPORTANT IS THIS?

"I know of no severe depression, in any country or any time, that was not accompanied by a sharp decline in the stock of money, and equally of no sharp decline in the stock of money that was not accompanied by a severe depression."

MILTON FRIEDMAN

WHY WOULD ANYONE WANT TO CAUSE AN ECONOMIC DEPRESSION? BECAUSE REAL WEALTH DOESN'T DISAPPEAR IN A DEPRESSION, IT IS ONLY REDISTRIBUTED. JUST TAKE A LOOK AT THIS LETTER FROM THE AMERICAN BANKER'S ASSOCIATION, A PREDECESSOR OF THE FEDERAL RESERVE, TO PRIVATE BANKERS IN 1891:

On September 1st, 1894, we will not renew our loans under any consideration. On September 1st, we will demand our money. We will foreclose and become mortgagees in possession. We can take two-thirds of the farms west of the Mississippi, and thousands of them east of the Mississippi as well, at our own price... Then the farmers will become tenants as in England.

ON DECEMBER 23, 1913, AFTER MOST SENATORS HAD GONE HOME FOR THE HOLIDAYS, THINKING THAT THE CONGRESSIONAL SESSION WAS CLOSED, A HANDFUL OF SENATORS RATIFIED THE CREATION OF THE FEDERAL RESERVE. THE ACT ITSELF HAD BEEN CONCEIVED IN SECRET BY A GROUP OF PRIVATE BANKERS. A NEW NATIONAL INCOME TAX PROGRAM WAS IMPLEMENTED IN AMERICA TO COINCIDE WITH THE CREATION OF THE FEDERAL RESERVE, IN ORDER TO PAY OFF THE INTEREST ON THE MASSIVE DEBT THIS PRIVATE ENTERPRISE WOULD CREATE.

SOME POLITICIANS REALIZED WHAT HAD HAPPENED.

"The financial system... has been turned over to... the Federal Reserve Board. That board administers the finance system by authority of... a purely profiteering group. The system is private, conducted for the sole purpose of obtaining the greatest possible profits from the use of other people's money... This Act establishes the most gigantic Trust on earth. When the President signs this bill, the invisible government by the Monetary Power will be legalized. The people may not know it immediately, but the day of reckoning is only a few years removed... The worst legislative crime of the ages is perpetrated by this banking bill."

Rep. Charles A. Lindbergh (R-MN)

"We have in this country one of the most corrupt institutions the world has ever known. I refer to the Federal Reserve Board. This evil institution has impoverished... the people of the United States... and has practically bankrupted our Government. It has done this through... the corrupt practices of the moneyed vultures who control it...

[It is] a super-state controlled by international industrialists acting together to enslave the world for their own pleasure."

BUT THE DAMAGE HAD BEEN DONE.

Rep. Louis McFadden (R-PA)

NOTES & FURTHER READING

PAGE 6

IN STRIKING CONTRAST TO CLAIMS MADE BY DEFENDERS OF THE OFFICIAL STORY THAT "CONSPIRACY THEORIES" DISHONOR THE DEAD, MANY OF THOSE WHO LOST LOVED ONES IN THE ATTACKS HAVE BEEN KEY FIGURES IN THE 9/11 TRUTH MOVEMENT. FOUR 9/11 WIDOWS WHO HAVE BECOME KNOWN AS THE "JERSEY GIRLS" TELL OF THEIR INCREDIBLE STRUGGLE TO UNCOVER THE TRUTH IN THE DOCUMENTARY, *9/11 PRESS FOR TRUTH*.

PAGE 7

WOODROW WILSON, *THE NEW FREEDOM: A CALL FOR THE EMANCIPATION OF THE GENEROUS ENERGIES OF A PEOPLE* (DOUBLEDAY, 1913)

PAGE 8

AMERICAN BANKERS ASSOCIATION LETTER
CONGRESSIONAL RECORD OF APRIL 29, 1913

FURTHER READING & VIEWING

JOHN R. ELSOM, *LIGHTNING OVER THE TREASURY BUILDING* (MEADOR PUBLISHING, 1941)

WILLIAM GRIEDER, *SECRETS OF THE TEMPLE* (SIMON & SCHUSTER, 1987)

G. EDWARD GRIFFIN, *THE CREATURE FROM JEKYLL ISLAND* (AMERICAN MEDIA, 1994)

ELGIN GROSECLOSE, *AMERICA'S MONEY MACHINE* (ARLINGTON HOUSE, 1980)

EMANUEL M. JOSEPHSON, *THE FEDERAL RESERVE CONSPIRACY AND ROCKEFELLER* (CHEDNEY, 1968)

PENNY LERNOUX, *IN BANKS WE TRUST* (ANCHOR PRESS/ DOUBLEDAY, 1984)

EUSTACE MULLINS, *THE SECRETS OF THE FEDERAL RESERVE, JEKYLL ISLAND EDITION* (BANKERS RESEARCH INSTITUTE, 1991)

SAM PIZZIGATI, *THE MAXIMUM WAGE* (APEX, 1992)

ANTONY SUTTON, *THE FEDERAL RESERVE CONSPIRACY* (CPA BOOK PUBLISHERS, 1995)

WICKLIFFE B. VENNARD, SR., *THE FEDERAL RESERVE HOAX* (OMNI PUBLICATIONS, 1973)

MASTERS OF THE UNIVERSE (52 MIN) <WWW.MADCOWPRESS.COM

THE MONEY MASTERS (210 MINUTES) <WWW.THEMONEYMASTERS.COM

"A DICTATORSHIP WOULD BE A HECK OF A LOT EASIER, THERE'S NO QUESTION ABOUT IT."

—GEORGE BUSH
BUSINESS WEEK, JULY 30, 2001

DON'T LOSE YOUR PLACE IN LINE...

CHAPTER TWO

A HISTORY OF BANKING
OR
THE REAL DECIDERS!

"WHILE MONEY DOESN'T TALK, IT SWEARS!"
—BOB DYLAN

"IT IS WELL ENOUGH THAT PEOPLE OF THE NATION DO NOT UNDERSTAND OUR BANKING AND MONETARY SYSTEM, FOR IF THEY DID, I BELIEVE THERE WOULD BE A REVOLUTION BEFORE TOMORROW MORNING."
—HENRY FORD

TO UNDERSTAND THE SCOPE OF THE FED'S POWER, AND TO UNDERSTAND HOW SUCH A SMALL GROUP OF PROFITEERING INDIVIDUALS COULD COME TO CONTROL THE FED, IT IS USEFUL TO TAKE A LOOK AT THE HISTORY OF BANKING.

IN MEDIEVAL EUROPE, THE FIRST BANKERS WERE GOLDSMITHS WHO STARTED SAFEKEEPING OTHER PEOPLE'S GOLD IN THEIR VAULTS. THE FIRST PAPER MONEY WAS ORIGINALLY JUST RECEIPTS FOR THIS STORED GOLD. PAPER MONEY CAUGHT ON BECAUSE IT WAS MORE CONVENIENT THAN CARRYING AROUND A HEAVY SACK OF METAL COINS.

EVENTUALLY, HOWEVER, GOLDSMITHS REALIZED THAT ONLY A SMALL FRACTION OF DEPOSITORS WOULD COME IN TO COLLECT THEIR GOLD AT ANY ONE TIME, AND THE SMITHS BEGAN TO CHEAT BY PRINTING MORE RECEIPTS THAN THEY ACTUALLY HAD ON DEPOSIT. THEY COULD THEN LOAN OUT THIS EXTRA "MONEY" AND COLLECT REAL INTEREST ON IT.

GOLDSMITHS FOUND THAT THEY COULD MAKE EVEN MORE PROFITS BY "ROWING" THE ECONOMY — EXPANDING OR CONTRACTING THE AMOUNT OF CURRENCY THEY PUT INTO CIRCULATION. WHEN LOANS WERE EASIER TO GET, PEOPLE WOULD BORROW MORE MONEY, BUT THEN THE SMITHS WOULD TIGHTEN THE MONEY SUPPLY, MAKING MONEY MORE DIFFICULT TO GET, AND SOME PEOPLE WOULDN'T BE ABLE TO PAY BACK THEIR LOANS.

THESE UNFORTUNATE FOLKS WOULD HAVE TO SELL THEIR HOMES OR BUSINESSES TO THE BANKS, COMMONLY FOR A FRACTION OF THEIR WORTH.

WHAT WERE ONCE CRIMES OF FRAUD AND USURY HAVE TODAY BECOME THE STANDARD LEGAL PRACTICES OF BANKS AROUND THE WORLD, GIVING THESE INSTITUTIONS ENORMOUS POWER OVER OUR ECONOMY! BACKING UP ONLY A FRACTION OF WHAT BANKS LOAN OUT IS KNOWN AS "FRACTIONAL RESERVE BANKING," AND MANIPULATING THE MONEY SUPPLY IS SIMPLY REFERRED TO AS "THE BUSINESS CYCLE."

BUT HOW DID PRIVATE BANKS GAIN SO MUCH POWER THAT ACTIONS WHICH WERE ONCE RIGHTLY CONSIDERED CRIMINAL HAVE NOW RECEIVED GOVERNMENT SANCTION? JUST REMEMBER THE GOLDEN RULE:

HE WHO HAS THE GOLD MAKES THE RULES

"Let me issue and control a nation's money, and I care not who writes the law."

AMSCHEL ROTHSCHILDE

AFTER QUEEN ELIZABETH I TOOK THE THRONE OF ENGLAND IN 1558, SHE TIGHTENED USURY LAWS AND BEGAN TO ISSUE GOLD AND SILVER COINS FROM THE PUBLIC TREASURY.

QUEEN ELIZABETH

Following Elizabeth, during the reign of King James, private bankers pooled their funds, and by 1642 they had gotten together enough money to finance the overthrow of his son Charles by Oliver Cromwell in the Puritan Revolution.

Religious struggles were the public focus of the war, but control of the money supply (public vs. private) was one major behind-the-scenes issue.

Though England was internally peaceful after the monarchy was restored in 1660, the expanding military adventurism of its kings kept the debts mounting. Bankers offered loans to first one side then the other, with profits assured by demanding that the victor honor the debts of the loser, a practice that continues to this day. The Parliament that reasserted itself in the Glorious Revolution of 1688 contained many of the money managers who were growing ever richer, and it saw no need to curtail the borrow-and-spend financing of an increasingly expensive military technology.

WITHIN A FEW YEARS THE TREASURY WAS BANKRUPT, BUT THE PRIVATE BANKERS WERE RICHER AND MORE POWERFUL THAN EVER. WHEN THE GOVERNMENT CAME TO THEM BEGGING FOR MORE LOANS, THE BANKERS RESPONDED BY DEMANDING THE CREATION OF THE FIRST PRIVATELY OWNED CENTRAL BANK, THE BANK OF ENGLAND, CHARTERED IN 1694. THE NEW DEBT-BASED ECONOMY REQUIRED INCREASED TAXATION OF THE BRITISH PUBLIC, AND, LATER, OF THE AMERICAN COLONISTS.

AT THIS TIME, THE COLONIES WERE ISSUING THEIR OWN MONEY, BASED ON NOTHING BUT GOOD FAITH, CALLED COLONIAL SCRIP. UNDER PRESSURE FROM THE BANK OF ENGLAND, THE BRITISH PARLIAMENT OUTLAWED COLONIAL SCRIP AND FORCED THE COLONIES TO USE MONEY BACKED BY GOLD, WHICH THE PRIVATE EUROPEAN BANKS MONOPOLIZED.

ACCORDING TO BENJAMIN FRANKLIN, IT WAS DENYING THE COLONIES THE RIGHT TO ISSUE THEIR OWN MONEY, NOT PETTY TAXATION, WHICH WAS THE PRIMARY CAUSE OF THE AMERICAN REVOLUTION. OTHER FOUNDING FATHERS AGREED. THOMAS JEFFERSON BELIEVED THAT BANKING INSTITUTIONS WERE MORE DANGEROUS TO OUR LIBERTIES THAN STANDING ARMIES.

"If the American people ever allow private banks to control the issue of their currency, first by inflation, then by deflation, the banks and the corporations which grow up around them will deprive the people of all property!"

Jefferson

AFTER THE REVOLUTION, HOWEVER, THE AMERICAN ECONOMY LAY IN RUINS. THE COLONIAL GOVERNMENTS HAD BEEN FORCED TO PRINT MORE AND MORE COLONIAL SCRIP IN ORDER TO PAY FOR WAR SUPPLIES, UNTIL THE BILLS HAD BECOME VIRTUALLY WORTHLESS.

A cartload of cash will hardly buy a cartload of food these days!

THE BANK OF NORTH AMERICA

DESPERATE FOR A NEW MONEY SYSTEM, CONGRESS ALLOWED ROBERT MORRIS TO OPEN A PRIVATE CENTRAL BANK IN 1781. MORRIS WAS A RICH MAN WHO HAD GROWN RICHER DEALING IN WAR GOODS DURING THE REVOLUTION. THE NEW BANK OF NORTH AMERICA WAS MODELED DIRECTLY AFTER THE BANK OF ENGLAND.

IN 1785, HOWEVER, THE CHARTER FOR THE BANK WAS NOT RENEWED, BECAUSE THE PEOPLE AND THE CONGRESS SAW CLEARLY THAT MORRIS WAS RUNNING IT WITH ONLY HIS OWN INTERESTS IN MIND.

Morris

BUT WITH THE HELP OF THOMAS WILING AND ALEXANDER HAMILTON, A CHARTER FOR THE FIRST BANK OF THE UNITED STATES WAS RAMMED THROUGH CONGRESS A MERE SIX YEARS LATER. THIS WAS AN EXACT COPY OF THE PREVIOUS BANK, WITH THE SAME PEOPLE IN CHARGE.

WHENEVER THE BANKS WERE THREATENED WITH LOSING THEIR CHARTERS, THEY FOUGHT FIERCELY, EVEN THREATENING TO CAUSE DEPRESSIONS.

"Nothing but widespread suffering will produce any effect on Congress... Our only safety is in pursuing a steady course of firm restriction-and I have no doubt that such a course will ultimately lead to restoration of the currency [to private bank control] and the re-charter of the bank."

Nicholas Biddle

BIDDLE MADE GOOD ON HIS THREAT DURING THE ANTI-BANK PRESIDENCY OF ANDREW JACKSON, BUT WAS FOUND OUT, ARRESTED, AND TRIED FOR FRAUD. SOON AFTERWARDS CAME AN ATTEMPT ON JACKSON'S LIFE WHICH, HOWEVER, FAILED. LATER, OTHER PRESIDENTS WHO OPPOSED THE ELITE CLIQUE WERE NOT SO LUCKY.

THE SECRET SOCIETY SYSTEM AT YALE GOES BACK TO THE LATE 1700S AND HAS SEEN MANY OF ITS INITIATES HOLD TOP OFFICES IN GOVERNMENT, EDUCATION, RELIGION, INDUSTRY, MEDIA AND FINANCE. THESE LEADERS THEN TRADITIONALLY APPOINT FELLOW MEMBERS TO POWERFUL POSITIONS, WHO IN *LOCK STEP* HIRE OTHERS. STANDING ON THE LEFT NEXT TO THE CLOCK, IN THE 1948 ''CELL,'' IS FUTURE CIA DIRECTOR AND PRESIDENT OF THE U.S., GEORGE H.W. BUSH, WHOSE FATHER AND FELLOW BONESMAN SENATOR PRESCOTT BUSH HAD HELPED TO FINANCE THE NAZI WAR MACHINE. SEVERAL COMPANIES PRESCOTT MANAGED WERE TAKEN OVER BY THE U.S. ALIEN PROPERTY OFFICE UNDER THE TRADING WITH THE ENEMY ACT IN 1942. THIS FACT WAS ''QUIETLY MANAGED'' THROUGH THE BONES-DOMINATED ''FREE'' PRESS, ALLOWING HIM TO BECOME THE U.S. SENATOR FROM CONNECTICUT IN A SPECIAL ELECTION IN 1952.

CHAPTER THREE
THE BROTHERHOOD OF DEATH

AS THE INDUSTRIAL AGE CAME INTO BLOOM, THE ELITES REALIZED THAT THEY WOULD NEED TO CONTROL TWO THINGS IF THEIR FAMILIES WERE TO REMAIN IN POWER. THE FIRST OF THESE WAS OIL, NEEDED TO PROVIDE THE EVER-EXPANDING ENERGY NEEDS OF AN EVER-EXPANDING ECONOMY. THE SECOND OF THESE WAS DRUGS, THE ROLE OF WHICH WILL BE EXPLORED LATER. IT ISN'T CLEAR IF THE BANKING FAMILIES EXPLICITLY CREATED SKULL & BONES TO MANAGE OIL AND DRUGS, OR IF THE ORDER WAS ASSIMILATED AFTER ITS EARLY MEMBERS FOUND SUCCESS IN THESE ARENAS, BUT WHICHEVER THE CASE, THE SECRET SOCIETY SOON BECAME A PIVOTAL PART OF THE ELITES' CONTROL NETWORK.

THE ORDER OF SKULL & BONES BEGAN AT YALE IN 1832, AS THE SECOND CHAPTER OF A GERMAN SECRET SOCIETY WITH WHICH ITS FOUNDERS HAD COME IN CONTACT WHILE STUDYING ABROAD. THESE STUDENTS WERE FASCINATED WITH THE NEW SCIENTIFIC METHODS OF PROPAGANDA AND MASS PSYCHOLOGY, AND BASED THE ORDER'S TEACHINGS ON THOSE OF THE GERMAN PHILOSOPHER HEGEL, WHO TAUGHT THAT THE STATE WAS ABSOLUTE AND THE INDIVIDUAL MEANINGLESS.

LOCATED IN NEW HAVEN, CONN., THE ORDER'S FORTUNES WERE BASED ON THE WEALTH OF THE COUSIN OF ONE OF ITS FOUNDING MEMBERS, WILLIAM H. RUSSELL. SAMUEL RUSSELL HAD BEEN THE PRIMARY AMERICAN PLAYER IN THE ''CHINA TRADE,'' OR OPIUM SMUGGLING. MANY OTHER GREAT AMERICAN AND EUROPEAN FORTUNES WERE BUILT ON THIS TRADE AS WELL, AS OPIUM BECAME THE MOST VALUABLE COMMODITY ON THE PLANET IN THE 1830s.

DR. BENJAMIN SILLIMAN JR., A BONESMAN, WAS THE FIRST TO MAKE THE PETROCHEMICALS GASOLINE AND PARAFFIN. HE CONFERRED WITH HIS COLLEAGUES, THEN MADE A REPORT TO THE PENNSYLVANIA ROCK OIL COMPANY, THE VERY FIRST OIL COMPANY.

"Gentlemen, it appears to me that your company may have in their possession a raw material from which by a simple and not expensive process, they may manufacture very valuable products."

Silliman

THE PENNSYLVANIA ROCK OIL COMPANY SOON PASSED INTO THE HANDS OF NEW HAVEN INVESTORS, AND THE COMPANY'S ORIGINAL OWNERS AND FINANCIERS, THE BISSELLS AND THE TOWNSENDS, SOON HAD THEIR SONS ENROLLED AT YALE AND IN SKULL & BONES.

Waite

In 1886, Supreme Court Chief Justice Morrison R. Waite, a Bonesman, made a decision regarding the 14th Amendment, which had been designed to protect freed black slaves. Waite ruled that the amendment applied to commercial corporations — that a corporation could now claim the legal rights and privileges of a person!

Incidentally, in the 1800s, Connecticut became known as the "Arsenal of Democracy," as more per capita defense spending went to it than any other state in the union. Connecticut is the birthplace of the Military-Industrial-Intelligence Complex.

"In the councils of government, we must guard against the acquisition of unwanted influence, whether sought or unsought, by the military industrial complex. The potential for the disastrous rise of misplaced power exists and will persist."

Eisenhower

When Rudolf Diesel showcased his new engine at the 1900 Exposition, it presented a major threat to the Oil Monopoly, because the Diesel engine was originally designed to run on peanut oil.

Diesel

But in 1913, Diesel mysteriously decided to "go for a swim" while on a ship crossing the English Channel, and within 20 years his engine was running solely on petrochemicals.

SKULL & BONES HAS INFLUENCED MANY IMPORTANT AMERICAN INSTITUTIONS. AFTER COMING TO DOMINATE THE YALE LEADERSHIP, SKULL & BONES MEMBERS WOULD GO ON TO BE THE FIRST PRESIDENTS OF THE UNIVERSITY OF CALIFORNIA, JOHNS HOPKINS, AND CORNELL. THEY HELPED TO FOUND AND SET THE DIRECTION FOR THE CARNEGIE INSTITUTION, THE PEABODY, SLATER, AND RUSSELL SAGE FOUNDATIONS, AS WELL AS THE AMERICAN ECONOMIC ASSOCIATION, THE AMERICAN HISTORICAL ASSOCIATION, AND THE AMERICAN PSYCHOLOGICAL ASSOCIATION.

BONESMEN GILMAN, WHITE, AND J.D. ROCKEFELLER HAD CONSIDERABLE INFLUENCE ON THE DEVELOPMENT OF PUBLIC EDUCATION.

Philanthropists lead the wa

DANIEL GILMAN

Born in Norwich, Connecticut, Gilman graduated from Yale College in 1852 with a degree in geography. At Yale he was a classmate of Andrew Dickson White, who would later serve as first president of Cornell University. The two were members of the Skull and Bones secret society, and would remain close friends.

After serving as attaché of the United States legation at St. Petersburg, Russia from 1853 to 1855, he returned to Yale and was active in planning and raising funds for the founding of Sheffield Scientific School.

ANDREW DICKSON WHITE

At the time of Cornell's founding, White announced that it would be "an asylum for Science—where truth shall be sought for truth's sake, not stretched or cut exactly to fit Revealed Religion" (Lindberg and Numbers 1986, pp. 2-3). Up to that time, American universities were exclusively religious institutions, and generally focused on the liberal arts and religious training (though they were not explicitly antagonistic to science).

In 1869 White gave a lecture on "The Battle-Fields of Science", arguing that history showed the negative outcomes resulting from

JOHN D. ROCKEFELL

From his very first paycheck, Rockefeller tithed ten percent to his church. As his wealth grew, so did his giving, prompted and public health causes, but also for basic science and the promulgated by Frederick T. Gates after 1891, and, after 1897,

Rockefeller believed in the Efficiency Movement, arguing that efficient, ill-located, unnecessary school is a waste... it is high enough trustees has been squandered on onwise educational built up a national system of higher education adequate to money had been properly directed to that end."

FOR THOSE WHO WOULD DOWNPLAY THE ROLE OF SKULL & BONES IN THE DEVELOPMENT OF THE UNITED STATES, CONSIDER THAT MEMBERS OF THIS ORDER HAVE THEREFORE DESIGNED THE INSTITUTIONS WHICH HAVE BEEN RESPONSIBLE FOR TEACHING AMERICANS THEIR HISTORY, DEFINING SANITY AND NORMALCY, AND TELLING AMERICANS WHAT AND HOW TO THINK.

SCORES OF BONESMEN CAN BE TRACED TO CIRCLES OF ENORMOUS INFLUENCE, INCLUDING THE FEDERAL RESERVE AND THE COUNCIL ON FOREIGN RELATIONS. THEY ARE CAPTAINS OF INDUSTRY, AND SERVE IN ALL BRANCHES OF THE POLITICAL APPARATUS. IT SHOULD BE NOTED THAT MANY SKULL & BONES MEMBERS NEVER ACHIEVE ANY GREAT PROMINENCE. BUT IT IS THIS WAY WITH EVERY SECRET SOCIETY — THERE HAVE TO BE A NUMBER OF "PORCH BRETHREN," LENDING AN AIR OF NORMALCY AND RESPECTABILITY, AND UNAWARE OF THE DESIGNS OF THE "INNER CIRCLE."

STICK TO YOUR DAILY ROUTINE. EVERYTHING IS UNDER CONTROL.

THE ACTIONS OF THE DOMINANT FAMILIES IN SKULL & BONES REVEAL A COMMON AGENDA, A REFINEMENT AND EXPANSION OF AN AGENDA HELD BY THEIR PREDECESSORS: POWER AND PROFIT AT ANY COST, EVEN IF THAT MEANS WAR, FAMINE, AND DISEASE FOR THE REST OF US. FOR SKULL & BONES HAS ADDED A NEW POLITICAL OBJECTIVE — A HEGELIAN SUPER-STATE, A "NEW WORLD ORDER" (TO USE THEIR OWN TERM), IN DIRECT CONTRADICTION TO THE VISION HELD BY THE FOUNDING FATHERS.

THIS NEW WORLD ORDER WOULD BE THE SYNTHESIS RESULTING FROM CONFLICTS BETWEEN OPPOSING EXTREMES, WHICH THEY THEMSELVES WOULD FINANCE AND INFLUENCE. THIS WAS THE HEGELIAN "HISTORICAL DIALECTIC" BEING USED TO IMPROVE UPON THE OLD METHODS OF THE BANKING FAMILIES.

"We are on the verge of a global transformation. All we need is the right major crisis and the country will accept the New World Order."

David Rockefeller

DURING HITLER'S RISE TO POWER, NAZI GERMANY RECEIVED MAJOR FINANCIAL HELP FROM MEMBERS OF SKULL & BONES, INCLUDING PRESCOTT BUSH. THROUGH BROWN BROTHERS HARRIMAN & CO., THE UNION BANKING CORPORATION, AND HAMBURG AMERICA SHIPPING LINES, BUSH AND OTHER BONESMEN HELPED GERMAN INDUSTRIALIST FRITZ THYSSEN BUILD THE NAZI WAR MACHINE. OF ALL THE WAR MATERIALS WHICH THE GERMAN MILITARY USED, THE PERCENTAGE WHICH CAME FROM THYSSEN IS ASTOUNDING.

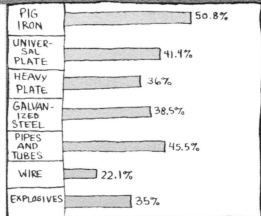

Material	Percentage
PIG IRON	50.8%
UNIVERSAL PLATE	41.4%
HEAVY PLATE	36%
GALVANIZED STEEL	38.5%
PIPES AND TUBES	45.5%
WIRE	22.1%
EXPLOSIVES	35%

A NUMBER OF MAJOR U.S. CORPORATIONS, INCLUDING IBM, FORD, AND COCA-COLA ALSO MAINTAINED PROFITABLE BUSINESS ARRANGEMENTS WITH THE NAZIS. IBM'S CONTRIBUTION WAS THE CREATION OF THE PUNCH-CARD SYSTEM USED TO KEEP TRACK OF GERMANY'S UNDESIRABLES AS THEY WERE BEING PROCESSED THROUGH THE DEATH CAMPS.

So IMPRESSED WERE AMERICAN CORPORATE LEADERS WITH HITLER'S POLITICAL SYSTEM, THAT, IN THE 1930S, A GROUP OF THEM PLANNED A COUP TO SET UP A SIMILAR SYSTEM IN AMERICA. THE COUP WAS TO BE LED BY RETIRED MARINE MAJOR GENERAL SMEDLEY BUTLER, WHO HAD SERVED CORPORATE INTERESTS FOR MANY YEARS BY SUPRESSING INDIGENOUS POPULATIONS IN THE PHILIPPINES AND CARIBBEAN. BUT...

BUTLER COOPERATED JUST LONG ENOUGH TO IDENTIFY AND EXPOSE THOSE BEHIND THE PLOT, INCLUDING THE DUPONT FAMILY, THE REMINGTON FAMILY, AND J.P. MORGAN, WHO WAS BACKED BY THE OLD EUROPEAN BANKING FAMILIES WHO HAD BONESMEN PARTNERS, AND WHO FINANCED MANY SKULL & BONES FAMILIES, INCLUDING THE ROCKEFELLERS AND HARRIMANS. ALL OF THIS CAME OUT IN THE INVESTIGATION BY THE MCCORMACK-DICKSTEIN COMMITTEE HEARINGS, THE TRANSCRIPTS OF WHICH ARE STILL PUBLICLY AVAILABLE.

"I was tired of being a gangster for capitalism!"

Butler

ALTHOUGH THE COMMITTEE SUPPORTED BUTLER'S ALLEGATIONS ABOUT THE PLOT, NO PROSECUTIONS OR FURTHER INVESTIGATIONS FOLLOWED. AT THE TIME OF HIS DEATH, BUTLER WAS THE MOST DECORATED U.S. MARINE IN HISTORY, WITH TWO MEDALS OF HONOR.

NOTES & FURTHER READING

SHORT LIST OF PROMINENT BONESMEN

BILL & JAMES, BUCKLEY - AUTHOR, CIA
MCGEORGE & BILL BUNDY - GOVERNMENT, CIA
G.H.W. & G.W. BUSH - OIL, GOVERNMENT, CIA
JOHN THOMAS DANIELS - ADM, INC. (GRAIN)
HENRY P. DAVISON - MORGAN GUARANTY TRUST
AVERELL HARRIMAN - INVESTMENT BANK, GOV.
ROLAND HARRIMAN - *NEWSWEEK* MAGAZINE
JOHN KERRY - GOVERNMENT
WINSTON LORD - GOVERNMENT
HENRY LUCE - *TIME/LIFE* MEDIA EMPIRE
EDWARD LAMPERT - KMART/SEARS
ARCHIBALD MACLIESH - POET, OSS
PERCY A. ROCEKFELLER - OIL, FINANCE
FREDERICK SMITH - FEDERAL EXPRESS
HAROLD STANLEY - MORGAN/STANLEY
HENRY STIMSON - GOVERNMENT
WILLIAM HOWARD TAFT - GOVERNMENT
FREDERICK WEYERHAUSER - TREES, PAPER, LAND

PAGES 16-21

L. VERNON BRIGGS, *HISTORY AND GENEALOGY OF THE CABOT FAMILY, 1475-1927* (1927)

MICHAEL HOFFMAN II, *SECRET SOCIETIES AND PSYCHOLOGICAL WARFARE* (WISWELL RUFFIN HOUSE 1989/1992)

MICHAEL HOWARD, *THE OCCULT CONSPIRACY: SECRET SOCIETIES — THEIR INFLUENCE AND POWER IN WORLD HISTORY* (DESTINY, 1989)

WALTER ISSACSON & EVAN THOMAS, *THE WISE MEN* (SIMON & SCHUSTER, TOUCHSTONE, 1988)

JOHN LOFTUS & MARK AARONS, *THE SECRET WAR AGAINST THE JEWS* (ST. MARTIN'S, 1994)

KRIS MILLEGAN, ET AL., *FLESHING OUT SKULL & BONES* (TRINEDAY, 2003)

ALEXANDRA ROBBINS, *SECRETS OF THE TOMB* (LITTLE & BROWN, 2002)

RON ROSENBAUM, "THE LAST SECRETS OF SKULL AND BONES" (*ESQUIRE*, SEPT. 1977)

CHARLES STEELE, *AMERICANS AND THE CHINA OPIUM TRADE IN THE 19TH CENTURY* (AYER 2001)

ALBERT STEVENS, *THE CYCLOPEDIA OF FRATERNITIES* (E. B. TREAT AND CO., 1907)

ANTONY SUTTON, *AMERICA'S SECRET ESTABLISHMENT* (TRINEDAY, 2002; LIBERTY HOUSE, 1986)

CARL A TROCKI, *OPIUM, EMPIRE AND THE GLOBAL POLITICAL ECONOMY* (ROUTLEDGE 1999)

PAGE 22

JULES ARCHER, *THE PLOT TO SEIZE THE WHITE HOUSE* (SKYHORSE PUBLISHING, 2007; HAWTHORN BOOKS, 1973)

SMEDLEY D. BUTLER, *WAR IS A RACKET* (FERAL HOUSE, 2003; NOONTIDE PRESS, 1984; ROUNDTABLE PRESS, 1984)

CHAPTER FOUR

SETTING THE STAGE

J.P. Morgan and his ''Robber Baron'' friends during the late 1800s began a consolidation of international commerce and capital, creating trusts and monopolies that continue today. The cabal's new oil business soon found vast new markets as the British, German and American navies all switched from coal to oil. With this leap in military technology came the predictable war, which has been related in American history books as being a consequence of Archduke Ferdinand's assassination. A much more reasonable explanation for the First World War emerges when you learn that the first place British troops deployed during WWI was Iraq. In addition to being the first oil war, World War I was a bigger opportunity for the bankers than they had ever experienced before. At the confilct's end conditions were ripe for more war, especially, with the same bankers again supplying money, managment and materials to opposing sides.

THE HISTORICAL RECORD SHOWS THAT THE US GOVERNMENT HAD CONSIDERABLE ADVANCE KNOWLEDGE OF THE ATTACK ON PEARL HARBOR. FDR DEVELOPED AN 8-POINT PLAN TO PROVOKE THE JAPANESE INTO ATTACKING TO GET AMERICAN SUPPORT FOR WWII. THE JAPANESE CODES HAD BEEN BROKEN. TOP OFFICIALS IN THE PHILIPPINES AND IN WASHINGTON, D.C. DID NOT GIVE A TIMELY WARNING TO ADMIRAL KIMMEL IN HAWAII. WITH A PREVIOUSLY AMBIVALENT PUBLIC NOW ENRAGED AT THE AXIS POWERS, THE UNITED STATES ENTERED WORLD WAR II, AND ADDED ENORMOUS SUMS TO THE DEBT OWED TO CENTRALIZED PRIVATE BANKS.

Pearl Harbor

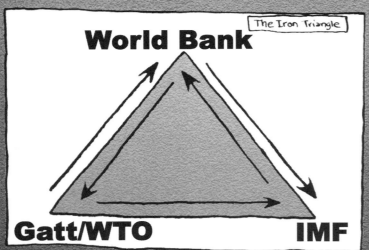

The Iron Triangle

World Bank

Gatt/WTO   **IMF**

WORLD WAR II SET THE STAGE FOR MANY SWEEPING CHANGES IN THE WORLD ECONOMIC AND POLITICAL SCENE. IN 1944, THE GENERAL AGREEMENT ON TRADES AND TARIFFS (GATT) WAS ENACTED, FOR THE STATED PURPOSE OF AIDING POST-WAR ECONOMIC RECOVERY. THE AGREEMENT PAVED THE WAY FOR CORPORATIONS TO EXPAND INTO TRANSNATIONAL ENTITIES. IN 1945, THE WORLD BANK WAS FORMED, CENTRALIZING PRIVATE BANKERS' POWER ON A GLOBAL LEVEL. AND IN 1947, THE INTERNATIONAL MONETARY FUND (IMF) BEGAN OPERATIONS.

COLLECTIVELY, THESE NEW GLOBAL FINANCIAL INSTITUTIONS WOULD WORK TO CONSOLIDATE WEALTH INTO FEWER AND FEWER HANDS. LOANS WERE OFFERED TO THIRD-WORLD NATIONS ONLY UNDER STRICT, AND OFTEN RADICAL, MANDATED CHANGES TO THEIR POLITICAL AND ECONOMIC STRUCTURE, SUCH AS REQUIREMENTS TO LET FOREIGN BUSINESSES AND INVESTORS PRIVATIZE PUBLIC SERVICES. AS OFTEN AS NOT, THE INTEREST ON THESE LOANS WOULD CREATE A DEBT WHICH SOON OUTWEIGHED THE HELP BEING RECEIVED FROM FIRST-WORLD COUNTRIES.

IN ANOTHER INTERESTING EPISODE AFTER THE WAR, OPERATION PAPERCLIP AND OTHER COVERT OPERATIONS BROUGHT NUMEROUS NAZI SCIENTISTS INTO AMERICA TO CONTINUE THE EXPERIMENTAL WORK THEY HAD BEEN PERFORMING FOR HITLER. THIS WAS RATIONALIZED AS A NECESSITY IN THE RACE FOR POWER AGAINST SOVIET RUSSIA, AND MANY WERE GIVEN KEY POSITIONS IN THE MEDIA AND ACADEMIA TO INFLUENCE AMERICAN THOUGHT. "EX-NAZIS" WERE ALSO USED TO TRAIN TORTURERS.

IN ADDITION TO DEVELOPING ROCKETS AND WEAPONRY, THIS WORK INCLUDED BRUTAL LSD EXPERIMENTS AIMED AT DEVELOPING A MEANS OF MIND-CONTROL, EFFORTS THAT BECAME COLLECTIVELY KNOWN BY THE CODE-NAME MK-ULTRA.

BUT THE FACT WAS THAT SOVIET RUSSIA HAD BEEN FINANCED BY WALL STREET AND SKULL & BONES ALL ALONG. STATE DEPARTMENT RECORDS SHOW THAT GUNS AND AMMUNITION WERE BEING SHIPPED TO THE BOLSHEVIKS LONG BEFORE WWII. COMPANIES CONTROLLED BY BONESMEN OF THE HARRIMAN GROUP JUMP-STARTED RUSSIA'S CRITICAL OIL AND MANGANESE MINING OPERATIONS WITH MASSIVE INVESTMENTS OF MONEY AND MACHINERY. AND IN 1920, THE ANGLO-RUSSIAN CHAMBER OF COMMERCE WAS CREATED TO PROMOTE TRADE WITH RUSSIA, HEADED BY BONESMAN SAMUEL R. BERTRON.

THEN, ON OCTOBER 22, 1945, SECRETARY OF WAR ROBERT PATTERSON CREATED THE LOVETT COMMITTEE, CHAIRED BY ROBERT A. LOVETT, A BONESMAN, TO ADVISE THE GOVERNMENT ON POST-WWII INTELLIGENCE ACTIVITIES. WITH HIS BUSINESS PARTNERS, THE DULLES BROTHERS, LOVETT CREATED THE NEW U.S. INTELLIGENCE ORGANIZATION...

AS WE COME TO THE CIA, WE RETURN TO THE TOPIC OF DRUGS, AND WHY DRUGS ARE SUCH AN IMPORTANT PART OF THE ELITES' CONTROL NETWORK. AS IS BECOMING MORE COMMONLY KNOWN, THE CIA USES ILLEGAL DRUG SALES TO FUND COVERT OPERATIONS, AND HAS ALSO USED THEM TO SUBVERT ETHNIC GROUPS AND SOCIAL MOVEMENTS, LIKE THE BLACK PANTHERS IN THE 1960s.

IN 1982, THE ATTORNEY GENERAL RULED THAT NO CIA EMPLOYEE OTHER THAN A CASE OFFICER NEED BE REPORTED FOR DEALING DRUGS.

¡Dios Mio!

EVEN WHEN THE CIA DOES GET CAUGHT IN THE ACT, SAY WITH A C-130 CARGO PLANE IN MEXICO CITY FULL OF A BILLION DOLLARS WORTH OF COKE, NOTHING MUCH HAPPENS...

IT SEEMS THAT THE MAIN FUNCTION OF THE DRUG TRADE IS TO KEEP THE U.S. ECONOMY AFLOAT. SOMEWHERE IN THE RANGE OF $600 BILLION IN DRUG MONEY IS LAUNDERED THROUGH THE U.S. BANKING SYSTEM EVERY YEAR. JPMORGAN-CHASE, CITIGROUP, BANK OF AMERICA, AND FIRST UNION BANK HAVE ALL BEEN CAUGHT DOING IT, AND THEY CONTINUE TO DO IT. THE CORRUPTION OF THE U.S. MONEY SYSTEM IS BY NOW SO PERVASIVE THAT THE U.S. ECONOMY COULD COLLAPSE WITHOUT THESE ILLEGAL LIQUID ASSETS TO COVER THE LOW- OR NO-INTEREST LOANS AND DERIVATIVES THAT MANY CORPORATIONS NEED FOR CONTINUED EXPANSION.

WALL STREET IS THE CIA. THE CIA IS WALL STREET. THIS BECOMES CLEAR WHEN WE LOOK AT THE PLAYERS INVOLVED. WE'VE ALREADY MENTIONED THE DULLES BROTHERS. JOHN FOSTER DULLES WAS THE SECRETARY OF STATE TO EISENHOWER, AN OSS SPY, AND A STANDARD OIL EXECUTIVE. ALLEN DULLES WAS A CIA DIRECTOR AND, INCIDENTALLY, WAS ALSO THE STAFF DIRECTOR AND LEAD INVESTIGATOR OF THE WARREN COMMISSION. BOTH BROTHERS WERE PARTNERS IN THE WALL STREET LAW FIRM SULLIVAN AND CROMWELL, WHICH HAS REPRESENTED, AMONG OTHER CLIENTS, THE ENERGY GIANT ENRON.

John + Allen

BILL CASEY, REAGAN'S CIA DIRECTOR, WAS CHAIRMAN OF THE SECURITIES AND EXCHANGE COMMISSION UNDER NIXON, A WALL STREET LAWYER AND A STOCK TRADER. HE HELPED TO FOUND CAPITAL CITIES, WHICH IN MARCH OF 1985 BOUGHT OUT ABC.

Casey

STANLEY SPORKIN WAS CASEY'S RIGHT-HAND MAN IN THE CIA, AND HE HAD PREVIOUSLY SERVED ON THE SEC FOR 20 YEARS. DAVID DOHERTY, SPORKIN'S REPLACEMENT, LATER BECAME THE VICE PRESIDENT OF THE NEW YORK STOCK EXCHANGE.

Sporkin

Deutch

Krongard

JOHN DEUTCH RETIRED FROM HIS POST AS DIRECTOR OF THE CIA IN DECEMBER 1996 TO JOIN THE BOARD OF DIRECTORS OF CITIGROUP. AND THE CIA'S EXECUTIVE DIRECTOR AT THE TIME OF 9/11, A.B. "BUZZY" KRONGARD, WAS PREVIOUSLY THE CEO OF THE INVESTMENT BANK ALEX BROWN.

Kerry

Bush + Bush

THE INTELLIGENCE, FINANCE AND OIL COMMUNITIES HAVE LONG BEEN SATURATED WITH BONESMEN, INCLUDING, OF COURSE, JOHN KERRY, GEORGE W. AND GEORGE H.W. BUSH. ANOTHER IMPORTANT THING TO REMEMBER ABOUT THE CIA IS ITS TIES WITH THE MEDIA. FOR EXAMPLE, OPERATION MOCKINGBIRD WAS EXPOSED AS AN ONGOING CORRUPTION OF MAINSTREAM MEDIA, INCLUDING ACTUAL INFILTRATION BY CIA AGENTS. SPOOKS CALL MANAGED MEDIA "THE MIGHTY WURLIZTER." THIS ABILITY TO "PLAY" THE AMERICAN PUBLIC SERIOUSLY CURTAILS THE WATCHDOG FUNCTION OF OUR PRESS, ENSHRINED IN OUR CONSTITUTION.

FIGHTING FOR G.O.D. (GOLD, OIL & DRUGS)

WITH ALL OF THIS IN MIND, LET'S TAKE A LOOK AT SOME OF THE EVENTS LEADING UP TO AMERICA'S NEXT MAJOR WAR, IN VIETNAM. DURING THIS PERIOD, THERE WAS ALSO A GREAT DESIRE BY SOME PARTIES TO SEE A WAR WITH CUBA. FOLLOWING THE BAY OF PIGS DEBACLE CAME A PLAN CALLED OPERATION NORTHWOODS. DECLASSIFIED AND MADE PUBLIC IN RECENT YEARS UNDER THE FREEDOM OF INFORMATION ACT, THIS DOCUMENT, SIGNED BY THE HIGHEST MILITARY OFFICIALS IN 1962, DESCRIBED PLANS TO CARRY OUT TERRORIST ATTACKS AGAINST THE UNITED STATES AND BLAME THEM ON CUBA IN ORDER TO JUSTIFY A WAR.

Lyman Lemnitzer

INCLUDED WERE PLANS TO EXPLODE BOMBS, SHOOT INNOCENT AMERICAN CIVILIANS IN THE STREETS, AND DESTROY A REMOTE-CONTROLLED AIRCRAFT THAT WAS SUPPOSEDLY FULL OF COLLEGE STUDENTS OVER CUBAN AIRSPACE. LUCKILY, SECRETARY OF DEFENSE MCNAMARA OVERRULED OUR SENIOR MILITARY OFFICIALS AND VETOED THE PLAN, AND PRESIDENT KENNEDY PERSONALLY REMOVED LYMAN LEMNITZER AS CHAIRMAN OF THE JOINT CHIEFS OF STAFF. PRESIDENT FORD WOULD LATER FIND A NEW JOB FOR THE NORTHWOODS MASTERMIND ON HIS FOREIGN INTELLIGENCE ADVISORY COMMITTEE, PUTTING LEMNITZER IN CLOSE PROXIMITY TO TWO OTHER NOTABLE FIGURES: DONALD RUMSFELD AND DICK CHENEY.

KENNEDY WAS ASSASSINATED SOON AFTER THE NORTHWOODS AFFAIR, AND SIMPLY READING THE WARREN COMMISSION REPORT MAKES CLEAR THAT THE LEE HARVEY OSWALD STORY IS ENTIRELY IMPOSSIBLE. WHEN ASKED HOW ANYONE COULD BE EXPECTED TO BELIEVE SUCH A CONTRADICTORY REPORT, ALLEN DULLES GAVE A STARTLING RESPONSE:

"The American people don't read."

Allen Dulles

FOLLOWING THIS CAME THE GULF OF TONKIN INCIDENT, IN WHICH TWO NORTH VIETNAMESE GUNBOATS SUPPOSEDLY ATTACKED SOME AMERICAN DESTROYERS. BUT PAPERS MADE PUBLIC IN 2005 SHOW THAT INTELLIGENCE OFFICERS DELIBERATELY SKEWED THE EVIDENCE BEING PASSED ON TO POLICY MAKERS. THE EVIDENCE NOW AVAILABLE INDICATES THAT, IN FACT, THE ATTACK NEVER EVEN HAPPENED, BUT AT THE TIME IT PROVIDED THE PRETEXT NEEDED FOR A MASSIVE ESCALATION OF AMERICAN INVOLVEMENT IN VIETNAM.

It was horrible, sir, I saw it myself.

Spook

DURING THE VIETNAM WAR, A COLONEL LANSDALE TOOK OVER CONTROL OF THE "GOLDEN TRIANGLE" FROM THE FRENCH AND THEIR CORSICAN INTERMEDIARIES. LANSDALE BROUGHT IN SICILIAN MOBSTERS TO HELP HIM MANAGE WHAT IS ONE OF THE BIGGEST OPIUM-PRODUCING REGIONS IN THE WORLD.

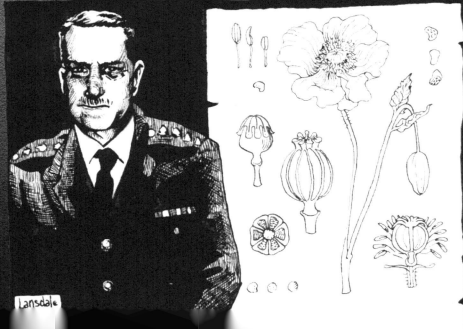

Lansdale

A READY MARKET WAS CREATED, AND THEN SENT HOME...

"It's that "Agent Orange"* shit again!"

* by Monsanto, who also made DDT.

TYCOON AND POLITICIAN ROSS PEROT WORKED ON A POW/MIA-FINDING MISSION AFTER THE WAR.

"I go in looking for prisoners, but I spend all my time discovering the government has been moving drugs around the world and is involved in illegal arms deals... I can't get at the prisoners because of the corruption among our own people."

Ross Perot

EVEN THOUGH BONESMAN GEORGE H.W. BUSH HAD SERVED ON THE BOARD OF DIRECTORS OF ELI LILLY, ONE OF THE LARGEST MAKERS OF THE PRECURSOR CHEMICALS NEEDED TO MANUFACTURE HEROIN AND COCAINE, AND ALSO THE COMPANY THAT FIRST SYNTHESIZED LSD FOR THE CIA, REAGAN PUT HIM IN CHARGE OF THE "WAR ON DRUGS." MANY WERE NOT IMPRESSED WITH HIS EFFORTS AS DIRECTOR OF THE NATIONAL NARCOTICS INTERDICTION SYSTEM.

"...an intellectual fraud... a liability rather than an asset."

Frances Mullen, Jr: Former Head of the DEA

THE IRAN-CONTRA AFFAIR WAS SUCH AN EGREGIOUS MISUSE OF CIA POWERS THAT IT BECAME THE BIGGEST POLITICAL SCANDAL OF THE 1980s. IT INVOLVED THE ILLEGAL SALE OF ARMS TO IRAN AND COCAINE TO THE AMERICAN PUBLIC, WITH FUNDS GOING TO SUPPORT RIGHT-WING PARAMILITARY GROUPS IN NICARAGUA. JOURNALIST GARY WEBB PUBLISHED ARTICLES ON THE COCAINE ASPECT OF THE DEAL. SOON ...

AROUND THIS SAME TIME, THE U.S. WAS SELLING CHEMICAL WEAPONS TO SADDAM HUSSEIN, AND AL-QAEDA, A LITTLE-KNOWN RELIGIOUS EXTREMIST GROUP LED BY OSAMA BIN LADEN, WAS RECEIVING TRAINING AND FUNDS FROM THE CIA AND ITS PAKISTANI COUNTERPART THE ISI, WHICH HAD BEEN CREATED BY THE CIA.

WHEN KUWAIT WAS ATTACKED BY IRAQ OVER ALLEGATIONS THAT KUWAIT WAS SLANT-DRILLING INTO IRAQ'S OIL FIELDS, AMERICAN PUBLIC SUPPORT FOR A GROUND WAR AGAINST IRAQ WAS AMBIVALENT UNTIL A SHOCKING VIDEO TESTIMONY BY AN "ANONYMOUS KUWAITI GIRL."

IN THE ENSUING PERSIAN GULF WAR, 135,000 IRAQIS WERE KILLED. AN ESTIMATED ONE MILLION WOULD GO ON TO DIE AS A RESULT OF TEN YEARS OF ECONOMIC SANCTIONS. BUT THE GIRL, WHO "COULD NOT BE IDENTIFIED FOR FEAR OF REPRISALS" TURNED OUT TO BE THE KUWAITI AMBASSADOR'S DAUGHTER. SHE HAD BEEN GIVEN HER LINES, AND WAS COACHED IN ACTING BY THE GIANT U.S. PUBLIC RELATIONS FIRM, HILL AND KNOWLTON. SEVERAL OTHER FAKE WITNESSES WERE TO FOLLOW IN A $10-MILLION PROPAGANDA CAMPAIGN.

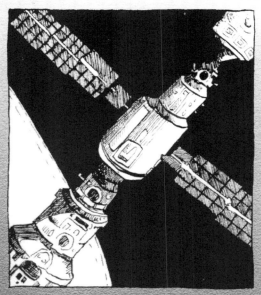

Importantly, Gulf War I was the first space war. The United States used its massive satellite network to identify and destroy 90% of Hussein's defenses very early in the war. The rest of the war was dragged out to put on a show. But it was clear that from this point on there was no conventional army in the world able to stand up to the U.S.

Here we see what is really at stake in all this.

"What is at stake is more than one small country - it is a big idea: A New World Order."

Bush Sr. 9-11-1990

The fake attacks and the march to consolidate power did not stop when the Democrats came into office with Bill Clinton. Emad Salem was an FBI informant in the 1993 World Trade Center bombing who thought he was participating in a sting operation until the FBI gave him real explosives. Concerned, he called his superiors in the Bureau and secretly recorded the conversation with the head of the FBI in New York.

Let the bombing take place!

Salem

It was later revealed that the bombers themselves had received training from U.S. Special Forces officer Ali Mohamed.

Good thing the American people don't read.

Spook

31

FIGHTING FOR G.O.D. (GOLD, OIL & DRUGS)

THE UNCHECKED POWER OF THE GROWING AMERICAN POLICE-STATE WAS VIVIDLY DEMONSTRATED THAT SAME YEAR. IN WACO, TEXAS, DAVID KORESH LED A RELIGIOUS GROUP KNOWN AS THE BRANCH DAVIDIANS. ALTHOUGH THE MEDIA TRIED TO PORTRAY KORESH AS A MANIACAL CULT LEADER WHO ABUSED CHILDREN, THERE IS NO REAL EVIDENCE FOR THIS.

"And besides, if child abuse was the real concern, how come we don't see Bradley tanks knocking down Catholic churches?"

Comedian Bill Hicks

THE FEDS CLEARLY WANTED TO SHOW OFF, BECAUSE THEY NOTIFIED LOCAL NEWS STATIONS THAT SOMETHING BIG WAS ABOUT TO HAPPEN. THIS SOON TURNED AGAINST THEM, HOWEVER, AS SOME OF THE BRANCH DAVIDIANS CHOSE TO RESIST THE TYRANNICAL ASSAULT ON THEIR COMPOUND WHICH FOLLOWED.

NEWS: Heroic Raids

AGAIN, THE MEDIA ADOPTED THE OFFICIAL GOVERNMENT LINE THAT THE DAVIDIANS THEMSELVES SET FIRE TO THEIR COMPOUND IN A CULTISH SUICIDE PACT, BUT LATER EVIDENCE REVEALED THAT THE FIRE WAS STARTED WHEN THE HUGE VOLUME OF CS GAS INJECTED INTO THE COMPOUND BY A TANK WAS IGNITED BY INCENDIARY FLARES LAUNCHED BY GOVERNMENT AGENTS.

oops.

Waco, Texas 1993

INFRARED OVERHEAD IMAGES OF THE SCENE BROUGHT OUT AN EVEN MORE DISGUSTING REVELATION. ON THE FAR SIDE OF THE PROPERTY, AWAY FROM THE NEWS CAMERAS, FEDERAL AGENTS MACHINE-GUNNED DOWN MEN, WOMEN, AND CHILDREN TRYING TO FLEE THE FLAMES. THE COMPOUND WAS QUICKLY DEMOLISHED AND BULLDOZED UNDER. JANET RENO AND HER CRONIES HAVE BEEN CAUGHT LYING OVER AND OVER AGAIN ABOUT THIS WHOLE INCIDENT, BUT TO THIS DAY, MOST AMERICANS HAVE ONLY HEARD THE FAKE COVER STORY.

Nothing to see here, folks.

PURPORTEDLY IN RETALIATION FOR THE WACO MASSACRE, TIMOTHY MCVEIGH SET OFF A TRUCK BOMB IN FRONT OF THE ALFRED P. MURRAH FEDERAL BUILDING IN 1995. HE WAS SUBSEQUENTLY TRIED AND EXECUTED AMIDST GREAT PUBLIC FANFARE.

McVeigh

1995: Oklahoma City

BUT LOCAL NEWS STATIONS TOLD THE STORY WHICH THE REST OF THE NATION NEVER HEARD. THE REAL DAMAGE TO THE BUILDING HAD COME FROM A NUMBER OF HIGHLY SOPHISTICATED DEVICES PLANTED INSIDE THE BUILDING. SOME OF THEM SURVIVED THE BLAST, AND WERE QUICKLY REMOVED BY BOMB SQUAD EXPERTS. MCVEIGH'S TRUCK BOMB LEFT AN INSIGNIFICANT CRATER IN FRONT OF THE BUILDING.

NEWS: Heroic Rescue

FEDERAL AGENTS WEREN'T AT THEIR OFFICES IN THE MURRAH BUILDING THAT DAY. INSTEAD, SOME WERE UP THE STREET, GETTING READY TO SWOOP DOWN ON THE SCENE IN THEIR FULL EMERGENCY GEAR.

Nothing to see here, folks.

BEFORE A THOROUGH INVESTIGATION OF THE BUILDING COULD BE CONDUCTED, IT WAS DEMOLISHED AND BURIED BY A COMPANY CALLED CONTROLLED DEMOLITION, INC. WHAT IS CLEAR FROM ALL OF THIS IS THAT MCVEIGH WAS SIMPLY USED AS A PATSY IN A GOVERNMENT-FUNDED OPERATION WHICH WAS USED TO JUSTIFY REPRESSIVE ANTI-TERRORISM LEGISLATION THE NEXT YEAR, AS WELL AS MASSIVE INCREASES IN THE ''BLACK OPERATIONS'' BUDGET.

DURING THIS TIME, AL-QAEDA CONTINUED TO QUIETLY RECEIVE U.S. FUNDS AND PROTECTION AS IT FOUGHT ON THE AMERICAN SIDE IN THE BALKANS IN 1999.

MEANWHILE, THE IMPERIAL ASPIRATIONS OF THE ELITES WERE AT WORK ABROAD AS THE NORTH AMERICAN FREE TRADE AGREEMENT WAS BROUGHT INTO EFFECT IN 1994. A TREATY BETWEEN CANADA, THE U.S. AND MEXICO, NAFTA FORCED MEXICO TO CHANGE ITS CONSTITUTION, REVOKING COMMUNAL LAND-RIGHTS FROM PEASANT FARMERS. WITH TARIFFS ALL BUT ELIMINATED, CHEAP, GOVERNMENT-SUBSIDIZED, GENETICALLY ENGINEERED CORN FROM HUGE U.S. AGRICORPORATIONS FLOODED THE MEXICAN MARKET.

Monsanto

FIGHTING FOR G.O.D. (GOLD, OIL & DRUGS)

THE PEASANT FARMERS HAD THEIR LIVELIHOOD DESTROYED, AND FOREIGN COMPANIES SOON BOUGHT UP THE NOW UNPROTECTED LAND TO INSTALL SWEATSHOPS. MANY OF THE FARMERS ENDED UP AS TENANTS ON THE LAND THEY HAD ONCE OWNED, AND HAD NO CHOICE BUT TO WORK IN THE MISERABLE CONDITIONS OF THESE "MAQUILLADORAS," COMMONLY MAKING $7 (U.S.) FOR A 14-HOUR DAY.

IN RESPONSE, THE ZAPATISTA ARMY OF NATIONAL LIBERATION ROSE UP FROM THE MOUNTAIN JUNGLES OF SOUTHEASTERN MEXICO. THEY HAVE EVER SINCE SERVED AS A MAJOR INSPIRATION FOR ANTI-CORPORATE-GLOBALIZATION ACTIVISTS AROUND THE WORLD.

NAFTA is a death sentence for the indigenous!

We choose to die fighting rather than die forgotten!

Marcos

THE WORLD TRADE ORGANIZATION REPLACED GATT IN 1995, AND HAS WORKED TO IMPOSE SIMILAR TRADE RULES ON NATIONS ACROSS THE GLOBE. DESIGNED BY CORPORATE LAWYERS, THE WTO HAS THE AUTHORIZATION TO OVERRULE NATIONAL LAWS WHENEVER THEY CONFLICT WITH CORPORATIONS MAXIMIZING THEIR PROFITS: THIS MEANS LAWS THAT PROTECT WORKERS, THE ENVIRONMENT, OR THE LOCAL ECONOMY.

THE WTO WOULD BE BROUGHT TO THE WORLD'S ATTENTION BY THE 1999 "BATTLE OF SEATTLE," WHERE PROTESTORS SUCCESSFULLY SHUT DOWN A MAJOR ROUND OF TRADE TALKS. SIMILAR MASSIVE PROTESTS ERUPTED IN QUEBEC CITY DURING A MEETING TO NEGOTIATE THE FREE TRADE AREA OF THE AMERICAS (FTAA), WHICH WOULD EXTEND NAFTA'S RULES TO ALL OF CENTRAL AND SOUTH AMERICA.

TOWARDS THE END OF THE CLINTON PRESIDENCY, PLAN COLOMBIA WAS PUT INTO EFFECT. THIS ACT SENT MERCENARIES IN DYNCORP PLANES TO SPRAY A SECRET INDUSTRIAL-STRENGTH VERSION OF MONSANTO'S ROUNDUP OVER LARGE PORTIONS OF THE COLOMBIAN COUNTRYSIDE IN A SUPPOSED EFFORT TO COMBAT COCA PRODUCTION. ALTHOUGH COCAINE IMPORTS TO THE U.S. HAVE ONLY INCREASED SINCE THE SPRAYING BEGAN, IT CONTINUES TO THIS DAY.

FIGHTING FOR G.O.D. (Gold, Oil & Drugs)

Why is this ineffective practice being continued?

Some have argued that the toxic spraying is aimed at quelling resistance by guerrillas who oppose the massive oil reserves in their country being drained by huge oil companies without benefiting the starving poor of Colombia.

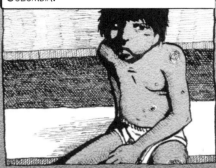

One of these oil companies was controlled by George W. Bush, an oilman who had found success only after investments from members of SBG, the Saudi Bin Laden Group.

Indeed, Bush would go on to expand Plan Colombia with the 2001 Andean Initiative. Although U.S. law prohibits military aid to countries with human rights records like Colombia, this didn't stop Bush from sending hundreds of millions of dollars, along with sophisticated military hardware, to the Colombian military, which in turn aids even more brutal right-wing paramilitary groups.

Human rights groups have recorded the sickening abuses of these paramilitaries, including slaughtering villagers with chainsaws in order to terrorize the rebellious population. Many of Colombia's most notorious military leaders studied at the School of the Americas, located at the U.S. Army's Fort Benning in Georgia.

Here they learned the art of assassination, torture, and the scientific repression of domestic uprisings. Tens of thousands have been killed or ''disappeared'' by SOA graduates.

Most Americans have heard very little of the history this book has presented so far. Why? Quite simply, every major news network is owned by people and corporations that profit from wars and/or the drug trade. The mainstream media has also been heavily infiltrated by the CIA through Project Mockingbird. And the influence of the Bonesman-founded American Historical Association and Bones-engendered foundation money helps keeps the ''historians'' in line and silent.

These elites are the people who control the transnational centralized private banks and transnational corporations, with a few ultra-powerful families and individuals leading the pack. Those at the very top are more powerful than most people can conceive. The economic activities of the most powerful transnational corporations dwarf the Gross Domestic Product of most nations. The three richest men in the world control more wealth than the poorest 47 nations combined.

NOTES & FURTHER READING

PAGE 25

Operation Paperclip

John Gimbel, *Science Technology and Reparations: Exploitation and Plunder in Postwar Germany* (Stanford University Press, 1990)

Lasby Clarence, *Project Paperclip: German Scientists and the Cold War* (Scribner's, 1975)

MK-Ultra

John Marks, *The Search for the Manchurian Candidate* (Times Books, 1979)

Carol Rutz, *A Nation Betrayed* (Fidelity Publishing, 2001)

PAGE 26

CIA C-130 cocaine smuggling

From the Wilderness 12/1998: <www.fromthewilderness.com/free/pandora/forest_service_c130s.html>; United States District Court, Northern District of Illinois, Eastern Division- No. 94CR0305, United States of America v. Luis Carlos-Herrera-Lizcano

$600 billion in drug money

DEA: <www.dea.gov/programs/money.htm>, *La Jornada* 3/12/2000, ''The United States, a Paradise for Money Launderers''; Senate Caucus on International Narcotics Control 3/4/04: <drugcaucus.senate.gov/moneylaundering04biden.html>

PAGE 27

CIA/Wall Street connections

Michael Ruppert, *Crossing the Rubicon* (New Society Publishers, 2004)

PAGE 28

Project NORTHWOODS

National Security Archive: <www.gwu.edu/~nsarchiv/news/20010430/index.html>; *New York Times* 11/19/97, ''Documents Show Pentagon's Anti-Castro Plots During Kennedy Years''; Reuters 11/19/97, ''Pentagon Planned 1960s Cuban 'Terror Campaign'''

"**T**HE VERY WORD 'SECRECY' IS REPUGNANT IN A FREE AND OPEN SOCIETY; AND WE ARE AS A PEOPLE INHERENTLY AND HISTORICALLY OPPOSED TO SECRET SOCIETIES, TO SECRET OATHS AND TO SECRET PROCEEDINGS. WE DECIDED LONG AGO THAT THE DANGERS OF EXCESSIVE AND UNWARRANTED CONCEALMENT OF PERTINENT FACTS FAR OUTWEIGHED THE DANGERS WHICH ARE CITED TO JUSTIFY IT.... AND THERE IS VERY GRAVE DANGER THAT AN ANNOUNCED NEED FOR INCREASED SECURITY WILL BE SEIZED UPON BY THOSE ANXIOUS TO EXPAND ITS MEANING TO THE VERY LIMITS OF OFFICIAL CENSORSHIP AND CONCEALMENT. THAT I DO NOT INTEND TO PERMIT TO THE EXTENT THAT IT'S IN MY CONTROL... "

—PRESIDENT JOHN F. KENNEDY
IN A SPEECH TO THE AMERICAN NEWSPAPER PUBLISHERS ASSOCIATION
WALDORF-ASTORIA HOTEL, NEW YORK, NY.
APRIL 27, 1961

NOTES & FURTHER READING

LEMNITZER SERVING W/ RUMSFELD & CHENEY
THE AMERICAN PRESIDENCY PROJECT <WWW.PRESIDENCY.UCSB.EDU/WS/INDEX.PHP?PID=5687

GULF OF TONKIN
NEW YORK TIMES 12/2/05, "VIETNAM WAR INTELLIGENCE 'DELIBERATELY SKEWED,' SECRET STUDY SAYS"

PAGE 30
GULF WAR DECEPTION
BARRIE ZWICKER, THE GREAT CONSPIRACY — THE 9/11 NEWS SPECIAL YOU NEVER SAW: <HTTP://WWW.GREATCONSPIRACY.CA/.>

PAGE 31
EMAD SALEM
NEW YORK TIMES 10/28/93, "TAPES DEPICT PROPOSAL TO THWART BOMB USED IN TRADE CENTER BLAST"

PAGE 32
WACO
WACO: THE RULES OF ENGAGEMENT, (164 MIN.)

PAGE 33
AL-QAEDA SUPPORT
OTTAWA CITIZEN 12/15/01, "BIN LADEN'S BALKAN CONNECTIONS"; DAILY TELEGRAPH 4/18/99, "SAS TEAMS MOVE IN TO HELP KLA 'RISE FROM THE ASHES'"

PAGE 34-35
PLAN COLOMBIA
AMNESTY INTERNATIONAL USA 6/21/2000, "AMNESTY INTERNATIONAL'S POSITION ON PLAN COLOMBIA"; HUMAN RIGHT'S WATCH: <WWW.HRW.ORG/CAMPAIGNS/COLOMBIA/ACTION/FACTSHEET.HTM>

SCHOOL OF THE AMERICAS
<WWW.SOAW.ORG>

ANDEAN INITIATIVE
THE CENTER FOR INTERNATIONAL POLICY 10/8/04, "CONGRESS DOUBLES THE LIMIT ON U.S. TROOPS IN COLOMBIA"; U.S. STATE DEPARTMENT: <USINFO.STATE.GOV/GI/ARCHIVE/2004/NOV/23-231491.HTML>

"**W**E ARE GRATEFUL TO THE WASHINGTON POST, THE NEW YORK TIMES, TIME MAGAZINE AND OTHER GREAT PUBLICATIONS WHOSE DIRECTORS HAVE ATTENDED OUR MEETINGS AND RESPECTED THEIR PROMISES OF DISCRETION FOR ALMOST FORTY YEARS.

"IT WOULD HAVE BEEN IMPOSSIBLE FOR US TO DEVELOP OUR PLAN FOR THE WORLD IF WE HAD BEEN SUBJECTED TO THE LIGHTS OF PUBLICITY DURING THOSE YEARS. BUT, THE WORLD IS NOW MORE SOPHISTICATED AND PREPARED TO MARCH TOWARDS A WORLD GOVERNMENT. THE SUPRANATIONAL SOVEREIGNTY OF AN INTELLECTUAL ELITE AND WORLD BANKERS IS SURELY PREFERABLE TO THE NATIONAL AUTO-DETERMINATION PRACTICED IN PAST CENTURIES."

—DAVID ROCKEFELLER
BILDERBERG MEETING, BADEN, GERMANY, JUNE 1991

FIGHTING FOR G.O.D. (Gold, Oil & Drugs)

Bohemian Grove Ritual

CHAPTER FIVE

END GAME?

"STOP THROWING THE CONSTITUTION IN MY FACE. IT'S JUST A GODDAMNED PIECE OF PAPER!"

—GEORGE W. BUSH
WHITE HOUSE, NOVEMBER 2005

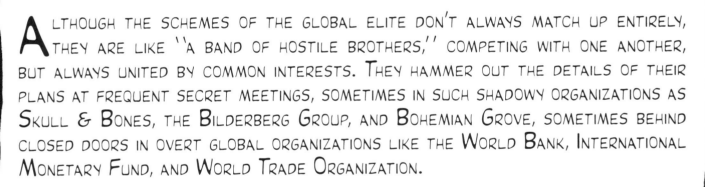

ALTHOUGH THE SCHEMES OF THE GLOBAL ELITE DON'T ALWAYS MATCH UP ENTIRELY, THEY ARE LIKE "A BAND OF HOSTILE BROTHERS," COMPETING WITH ONE ANOTHER, BUT ALWAYS UNITED BY COMMON INTERESTS. THEY HAMMER OUT THE DETAILS OF THEIR PLANS AT FREQUENT SECRET MEETINGS, SOMETIMES IN SUCH SHADOWY ORGANIZATIONS AS SKULL & BONES, THE BILDERBERG GROUP, AND BOHEMIAN GROVE, SOMETIMES BEHIND CLOSED DOORS IN OVERT GLOBAL ORGANIZATIONS LIKE THE WORLD BANK, INTERNATIONAL MONETARY FUND, AND WORLD TRADE ORGANIZATION.

The World Bank

THROUGHOUT THE CENTURIES, THE FAMILIES WHICH COMPRISE THE "ELITES OF THE ELITE" HAVE SHOWN UNPARALLELED CYNICISM AND CONTEMPT FOR THE REST OF US IN THEIR UNENDING QUEST TO CONSOLIDATE POWER INTO AS FEW HANDS AS POSSIBLE. THEY HAVE FINANCED WARS, ARRANGED FAKE ACTS OF TERRORISM, CAUSED HUGE ECONOMIC DEPRESSIONS, AND DRAINED ENTIRE COUNTRIES OF RESOURCES. WITH THIS IN MIND, THE EVENTS OF SEPTEMBER 11, 2001 APPEAR AS THE LOGICAL NEXT STEP, SHOCKING AND UNUSUAL ONLY IN THE IMMEDIATE DEATH AND DESTRUCTION THEY INFLICTED ON A COMPLACENT AMERICAN PUBLIC.

IN SEPTEMBER OF 2000, A DOCUMENT FROM THE NEOCONSERVATIVE THINK-TANK, "PROJECT FOR A NEW AMERICAN CENTURY," WHICH INCLUDED DICK CHENEY, DONALD RUMSFELD, JEB BUSH, AND PAUL WOLFOWITZ (FUTURE WORLD BANK PRESIDENT), OUTLINED A PLAN FOR "FULL-SPECTRUM DOMINANCE" OF WORLD AFFAIRS. BUT, THE REPORT LAMENTED, THE AMERICAN PEOPLE WOULD PROBABLY NOT GET BEHIND SUCH A PLAN...

"...ABSENT SOME CATASTROPHIC AND CATALYZING EVENT, LIKE A NEW PEARL HARBOR."

John O'Neill

A NUMBER OF INTELLIGENCE OFFICERS WERE INVESTIGATING AL-QAEDA BEFORE 9/11, BUT WHEN PRESIDENT BUSH SIGNED EXECUTIVE ORDER W-1991, THEY WERE ORDERED TO CEASE AND DESIST. JULIE SIRRS, COLEEN ROWLEY, SIBEL EDMONDS, RANDY GLASS, KEN WILLIAMS, ROBERT WRIGHT, AND OTHER INTELLIGENCE AGENTS COMPLAINED THAT INFORMATION THEY HAD UNCOVERED COULD HAVE PREVENTED THE ATTACKS. AGENT JOHN O'NEILL'S EFFORTS TO BE HEARD WERE REWARDED BY HIS BEING TRANSFERRED TO SECURITY AT THE WORLD TRADE CENTER, WHERE HE DIED HIS FIRST DAY ON THE JOB. DAVE FRASCA, HEAD OF THE FBI RADICAL FUNDAMENTALISM UNIT, QUASHED A NUMBER OF THESE REPORTS AND RECEIVED A PROMOTION.

A HOST OF FOREIGN INTELLIGENCE AGENCIES URGENTLY WARNED THE U.S. THAT THE 9/11 ATTACKS WERE IMMINENT, INCLUDING THOSE OF GERMANY, FRANCE, GREAT BRITAIN, RUSSIA, EGYPT, MOROCCO, AND, IN AUGUST OF 2001, OUR STAUNCH MID-EAST ALLY ISRAEL. SPECIFIC TARGETS AND THE DATE WERE NAMED. EVEN THE TALIBAN TRIED TO WARN THE U.S. THAT MONTH. "WE CLEARLY WARNED THEM," SAID THE HEAD OF RUSSIAN INTELLIGENCE, BUT THEY "DID NOT PAY THE NECESSARY ATTENTION."

"The information provided by European Intelligence services prior to 9/11 was so extensive that it is no longer possible for either the CIA or FBI to assert a defense of incompetence."

U.S. Federal Prosecutor John Loftus

UNITED STATES OFFICIALS COULD NEVER REALLY GET THEIR STORY STRAIGHT ON THIS POINT.

"There were lots of warnings."

Donald Rumsfeld

"No warnings."

Ari Fleischer

CERTAIN VIPs RECEIVED TRAVEL WARNINGS BEFORE 9/11. IN JUNE OF '01 ATTORNEY GENERAL ASHCROFT STOPPED FLYING COMMERCIAL FLIGHTS BECAUSE OF SECURITY CONCERNS. THE DAY BEFORE THE ATTACKS, TOP PENTAGON OFFICIALS CANCELLED FLIGHTS BECAUSE OF SECURITY CONCERNS. SAN FRANCISCO MAYOR WILLIE BROWN RECEIVED TRAVEL WARNINGS 8 HOURS BEFORE THE ATTACK.

Condoleeza Rice

Silverstein

SIX WEEKS BEFORE THE ATTACKS, LARRY SILVERSTEIN, WHO ALREADY OWNED WTC7, LEASED THE ENTIRE WORLD TRADE CENTER COMPLEX AND TOOK OUT A RECORD INSURANCE POLICY ON IT, WITH A SPECIAL CLAUSE SPECIFICALLY RELATING TO ACTS OF TERRORISM, WHICH WOULD ALLOW HIM TO COLLECT BILLIONS. SILVERSTEIN IS A REAL ESTATE TYCOON WITH DEEP POLITICAL CONNECTIONS. HE WAS THE SINGLE LARGEST CAMPAIGN DONOR TO HILLARY CLINTON DURING HER RUN FOR THE SENATE IN NEW YORK. HE WAS THE DRIVING FORCE BEHIND AN ATTEMPT TO SET UP A WTO-STYLE "FREE TRADE ZONE" IN ISRAEL, AND HAS BEEN ACCUSED OF LAUNDERING HEROIN MONEY THROUGH A CLUB HE OWNS. ON 9/11 HE WAS ABSENT FROM HIS OFFICE ON THE 88TH FLOOR OF THE NORTH TOWER BECAUSE OF A DOCTOR'S APPOINTMENT. BUSH'S COUSIN JIM PIERCE LIKEWISE ESCAPED DEATH BY A LAST-MINUTE CHANGE OF LOCATION FOR A BUSINESS MEETING.

RECORD NUMBERS OF "PUT OPTIONS" WERE PLACED ON AMERICAN AND UNITED AIRLINES IMMEDIATELY BEFORE THE ATTACKS, AS WELL AS SOME WTC-BASED COMPANIES. BASICALLY, THIS IS A STOCK MARKET MOVE IN WHICH YOU ARE BETTING THAT A COMPANY'S STOCK VALUE IS ABOUT TO PLUMMET. MUCH OF THIS TRADING WAS DONE THROUGH THAT VERY BANK WHOSE FORMER CHAIRMAN WAS A.B. KRONGARD, THE EXECUTIVE DIRECTOR OF THE CIA DURING 9/11.

THE SEC HAS NEVER RELEASED THE NAMES OF THOSE WHO PROFITED FROM THESE DEALS, AND THE 9/11 PANEL DECIDED THAT THIS COULDN'T HAVE CONSTITUTED FOREKNOWLEDGE, BECAUSE NONE OF THE PEOPLE INVOLVED HAD ANY CONCEIVABLE LINKS TO AL-QAEDA (NOTE THE CIRCULAR LOGIC).

Krongard

Just a lucky guess.

I had my tarot read.

BUT CLEARLY THERE WERE MANY PEOPLE WHO KNEW WHAT WAS COMING.

MEANWHILE SKULL & BONES MEMBER JONATHAN BUSH'S RIGGS BANK WAS LAUNDERING MONEY FOR TERRORISTS, FOR WHICH IT WAS FINED $25 MILLION IN 2004.

LET'S TAKE A LOOK AT THE OFFICIAL CULPRITS OF THIS CRIME. AUTHORITIES WERE QUICK TO POINT THE FINGER, EVEN BEFORE THE SECOND PLANE HAD CRASHED.

Good thing the American people don't read.

Osama bin Laden did it!

Wait for it!

NEW

D'oh!

As previously mentioned, bin Laden was a long-time CIA asset, codename Tim Osman. A number of curious facts raise the question of whether he still is. In July of 2001, it is reported that bin Laden, who had been wanted since 1998, underwent medical treatment at the American hospital in Dubai, where he was met by the local CIA chief.

In 1999 and 2000, the Taliban offered to turn him over to the U.S., an offer which was never taken up.

One of President Bush's first acts after coming into office in January of 2001 was to recall attack submarines which had been positioned for the prior two years within striking distance of Al-Qaeda bases in Afghanistan.

And it has been widely reported that in November of 2001, Osama bin Laden and his troops were repeatedly allowed to use obvious routes to escape from U.S. troops in Afghanistan. A shocking string of murders and suicides ensued among involved Special Forces soldiers after they returned to the U.S.

IN EARLY NOVEMBER, AN AL-QAEDA CONVOY OF AROUND 1,000 VEHICLES SOMEHOW MANAGED TO SLIP BY ALLIED FORCES TO ESCAPE FROM KABUL.

IN MID-NOVEMBER, ANOTHER MAJOR CONVOY MADE IT'S WAY FROM JALALABAD TO TORA BORA. A NEARBY AIRPORT WAS BOMBED, BUT THE CONVOY WAS LEFT UNTOUCHED.

We've got him surrounded on three sides.

Why don't they send us in?

CIA FIELD COMMANDER GARY BERNTSEN WAS OUTRAGED WHEN, AT THE BATTLE OF TORA BORA, BIN LADEN HIMSELF WAS PINNED DOWN BUT THEN ALLOWED TO ESCAPE.

AND LATE IN NOVEMBER, A MAJOR AIRLIFT CARRIED 4-5,000 AL-QAEDA FIGHTERS FROM KONDUZ INTO PAKISTAN, AN OPERATION WHICH ABSOLUTELY COULD NOT GO UNNOTICED. FOR MULTIPLE TRANSPORT JETS TO FLY UNMOLESTED THROUGH THIS TIGHTLY CONTROLLED AIRSPACE WOULD HAVE REQUIRED THE BLESSING OF BOTH THE PAKISTANI DICTATOR, GENERAL MUSHARRAF, AND DEFENSE SECRETARY DONALD RUMSFELD.

THE "SMOKING TAPE" IN WHICH OSAMA BIN LADEN GLOATS ABOUT 9/11 IS ALSO PROBLEMATIC. IT WAS A HOME VIDEO, SUPPOSEDLY FOUND IN AFGHANISTAN DURING A MILITARY RAID. IT IS OF POOR QUALITY, AND SHOWS SOMEONE WHO RESEMBLES BIN LADEN, BUT IS MUCH HEAVIER SET, HAS DISPROPORTIONAL FACIAL FEATURES, WEARS JEWELRY, AND WRITES A NOTE WITH THE WRONG HAND.

THEN THERE ARE THE HIJACKERS. *FUNDAMENTALIST MUSLIMS GONE WILD!* SHOULD HAVE BEEN A HEADLINE IN EVERY MAJOR NEWSPAPER, BUT WASN'T. MOHAMMED ATTA HAD A STRIPPER GIRLFRIEND IN FLORIDA, AND, ALONG WITH SOME OF THE OTHER ALLEGED HIJACKERS, IS KNOWN TO HAVE HAD AN OVERWHELMING APPETITE FOR LAP DANCES, ALCOHOL, AND PORK, ALL OF WHICH ARE FORBIDDEN IN ISLAM. IS THIS REALLY THE BEHAVIOR OF PEOPLE WHO ARE SO TOTALLY DEVOTED TO THEIR RELIGION THAT THEY'RE WILLING TO GIVE THEIR LIVES FOR IT?

MUCH OF THE EVIDENCE USED TO BLAME THESE MEN APPEARS TO HAVE BEEN FABRICATED. THE PASSPORTS, FOR INSTANCE, MIRACULOUSLY SURVIVED THE RAGING INFERNOS AT THE WTC AND PENTAGON, FIRES SO INTENSE THAT THEY SUPPOSEDLY CAUSED THE FORMER TO COLLAPSE AND VAPORIZED THE PLANE AT THE LATTER.

FIGHTING FOR G.O.D. (GOLD, OIL & DRUGS)

DESPITE BEING ON WATCH LISTS AND BEING MONITORED BY PROGRAMS LIKE ABLE DANGER, THE HIJACKERS RECEIVED NO TROUBLE FROM THE FBI. THEY MOVED IN AND OUT AND AROUND THE COUNTRY WITH EASE, PERHAPS BECAUSE 15 OF THEM HAD RECEIVED THEIR VISAS AT A CONSULATE IN SAUDI ARABIA THROUGH WHICH THE CIA RUNS A *SPECIAL PASS* PROGRAM FOR INTELLIGENCE ASSETS.

MOHAMMED ATTA ALSO LIKED TO GAMBLE...

ON A CRUISE SHIP...

OWNED BY DISGRACED REPUBLICAN LOBBYIST JACK ABRAMOFF.

Abramoff

THERE IS ALSO THE QUESTION OF WHETHER THESE MEN EVEN HAD THE ABILITY TO FLY THE HIJACKED PLANES. HANI HANJOUR, WHO SUPPOSEDLY PILOTED FLIGHT 77, WAS SUCH A BAD PILOT THAT HE COULD BARELY FLY A SMALL CESSNA, WHICH IS VASTLY SIMPLER THAN A MASSIVE 757. YET ON 9/11 HE SUPPOSEDLY PERFORMED SUCH A TIGHT SPIRAL TO HIT THE PENTAGON THAT SEASONED PILOTS DOUBTED THEY COULD DO IT.

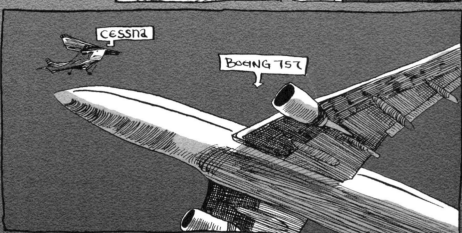

Cessna

BOEING 757

Ahmed

Goss

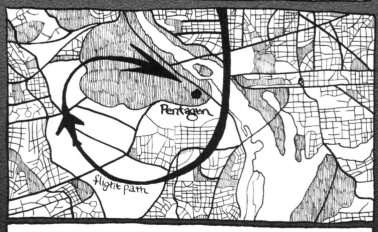

Pentagon

flight path

IT IS BECOMING MORE AND MORE EVIDENT THAT THE HIJACKERS WERE MERELY PATSIES, BEING MANIPULATED BY POWERS OF WHICH THEY KNEW NOTHING. SHORTLY BEFORE 9/11, MOHAMMED ATTA WAS WIRED $100,000 ON THE ORDER OF THE HEAD OF ISI, THE PAKISTANI INTELLIGENCE SERVICE SET UP BY THE CIA. AND YET, ON THE MORNING OF 9/11, THIS SAME GENERAL MAHMOUD AHMED WAS IN WASHINGTON, MEETING WITH TOP OFFICIALS, INCLUDING PORTER GOSS, CHAIRMAN OF THE HOUSE PERMANENT SELECT COMMITTEE ON INTELLIGENCE, WHO WOULD LATER BE PROMOTED TO HEAD OF THE CIA. WERE THEY GETTING THEIR STORIES STRAIGHT?

THE PENTAGON, IT SHOULD ALSO BE NOTED, IS PROBABLY THE MOST HEAVILY DEFENDED BUILDING ON THE FACE OF THE PLANET. IT IS SURROUNDED BY MISSILE BATTERIES DESIGNED TO SHOOT DOWN ANY APPROACHING OBJECT NOT BROADCASTING A FRIENDLY MILITARY TRANSPONDER SIGNAL. AND WHILE THE PLANE'S APPROACH PATH WOULD HAVE MADE IT EASY TO DIVE INTO THE SECTION OF THE PENTAGON HOUSING THE OFFICES OF RUMSFELD AND ALL OF THE TOP BRASS, THE PLANE HIT THE OPPOSITE SIDE OF THE BUILDING BY PERFORMING A MANEUVER SO DIFFICULT THAT AIR TRAFFIC CONTROLLERS ALL THOUGHT THEY WERE OBSERVING A MILITARY JET ON THEIR SCREENS.

WHAT WAS IN THIS SECTION? NEXT TO NOTHING OFFICIALS WOULD CONSIDER IMPORTANT... EXCEPT FOR ONE THING. JUST PRIOR TO THE 9/11 ATTACKS, RUMSFELD HAD QUIETLY ANNOUNCED THAT $2.3 TRILLION WAS MYSTERIOUSLY MISSING FROM THE PENTAGON BUDGET. THE FILES THAT COULD HAVE SHOWN WHERE THIS MONEY WENT WERE STORED IN THE SECTION DESTROYED.

Donald Rumsfeld

We could hit it here if we want to kill a few hundred civilians instead of a few thousand military officers.

PENTAGON

Better yet, we could forget the planes altogether and just use harsh language. *#@& you, Uncle Sam!

ATTA

Osama

THOSE THAT DIED AT THE PENTAGON WERE MOSTLY CIVILIAN CONSTRUCTION WORKERS, WHO HAD BEEN REINFORCING THAT SECTION OF THE BUILDING TO WITHSTAND JUST SUCH AN ATTACK. SINCE ALL OF THIS WAS PUBLIC KNOWLEDGE, ''TERRORIST MASTERMINDS'' WOULD HAVE SURELY KNOWN WHERE THE IMPORTANT TARGETS WERE.

SIMULATIONS WERE RUN BY NORAD IN 1999 IN WHICH HIJACKED AIRLINERS WERE ''FLOWN'' INTO THE WORLD TRADE CENTER AND PENTAGON, AND EXERCISES WERE RUN IN LATE 2000 AND EARLY 2001 BY THE PENTAGON WHICH SIMULATED A BOEING 757 CRASHING INTO THE BUILDING. CHARLES BURLINGAME, AN EX-NAVY F-4 PILOT, PARTICIPATED IN THESE LATTER EXERCISES BEFORE RETIRING TO TAKE A CIVILIAN JOB WITH AMERICAN AIRLINES, WHICH ENDED WHEN HE SERVED AS THE PILOT FOR THE PLANE THAT HIT THE PENTAGON. AND YET, AFTER THE ATTACKS...

"Generally it is impossible to carry out an act of terror on the scenario which was used in the U.S.A. yesterday... As soon as something like that happens here, I am reported about that right away and in a minute we are all up."

"I don't think anybody could have predicted that these people would take an airplane and slam it into the World Trade Center."

Condoleeza Rice

Gen. Anatoly Kornukov, Comander-in-Chief of Russian Air Force.

BUT REALLY, HOW COULD ANY OF THE PLANES HAVE GOTTEN ANYWHERE NEAR THEIR TARGETS?

STANDARD OPERATING PROCEDURES REQUIRE JETS TO SCRAMBLE TO INTERCEPT ANY OFF-COURSE AIRCRAFT. THIS IS AN ENTIRELY ROUTINE OPERATION, AND NORMALLY HAPPENS WITHIN 20 MINUTES. INDEED, IN THE YEAR BEFORE 9/11, IT WAS CARRIED OUT FLAWLESSLY 67 TIMES. SO HOW COULD IT FAIL FOUR TIMES IN A ROW ON 9/11, ESPECIALLY WITH A 90-MINUTE GAP BETWEEN THE FIRST AND LAST PLANE CRASHES? WITHOUT ANY EXPLANATION, TOP OFFICIALS HAVE CHANGED THEIR STORIES ABOUT THE EXACT TIMES OF VARIOUS EVENTS ON A NUMBER OF OCCASIONS. BUT THE NUMBERS JUST DON'T ADD UP, ANY WAY YOU LOOK AT IT.

"When the news came out I had to wonder. why did airplanes fly around for an hour and a half without interceptors being scrambled from Andrews? Why did the president just sit in the schoolroom when he heard the news?"

Paul Hellyer, former Canadian Minister of Defense.

INDEED, GIVEN THAT HE MIGHT HAVE BEEN A POSSIBLE TARGET, IT WOULD HAVE BEEN THE SECRET SERVICE'S DUTY TO RUSH THE PRESIDENT TO SAFETY... UNLESS IT WAS KNOWN THAT HE *WASN'T* A TARGET.

SO WAS THERE A STAND-DOWN ORDER? ACTUALLY, IT TURNS OUT THAT A STAND-DOWN ORDER WASN'T NECESSARY BECAUSE OF A LITTLE SOMETHING DICK CHENEY HAD COOKED UP. ON 9/11, CHENEY WAS DIRECTING NUMEROUS WAR GAMES WHICH COMPLETELY DISABLED OUR AIR RESPONSE. MANY OF THE JETS USUALLY PROTECTING THE EASTERN SEABOARD HAD BEEN SENT TO ALASKA AND NORTHWEST CANADA TO PARTICIPATE IN A MOCK RUSSIAN-INVASION DRILL. THOSE THAT REMAINED WERE LEFT TO CHASE PHANTOM RADAR BLIPS WHICH HAD BEEN INSERTED ONTO SCREENS AS PART OF A DRILL SIMULATING HIJACKINGS.

FAA: "WE HAVE A PROBLEM HERE. WE HAVE A HIJACKED AIRCRAFT HEADED TOWARDS NEW YORK, AND WE NEED YOU GUYS TO... WE NEED SOMEONE TO SCRAMBLE SOME F-16S OR SOMETHING TO HELP US OUT."

NORAD: "Is this real world, or exercise?"

FAA: "NO, THIS IS NOT AN EXERCISE, NOT A TEST."

THANKS TO THESE DIVERSIONS, THERE WERE MORE POSSIBLE HIJACKINGS THAN WE HAD FIGHTERS LEFT TO INVESTIGATE. CONFLICTING ORDERS SENT OUT BY THE COMMAND CENTER OVERSEEN BY CHENEY AND THE SECRET SERVICE DIDN'T HELP EITHER.

"What I saw on September 11 was a perfectly executed act that could only have been performed with the help of intelligence services!"

Andreas Von Bülow

THERE ARE ALSO A NUMBER OF ANOMALIES IN REGARDS TO THE ATTACKS THEMSELVES. EVIDENCE HAS LED SOME TO SPECULATE THAT THE JETLINERS WERE AT SOME POINT TAKEN OVER VIA REMOTE CONTROL. ONE COMPANY WHICH PRODUCES SUCH TECHNOLOGY IS SYSTEM PLANNING CORPORATION, WHICH COUNTED DOV ZAKHEIM AS A FORMER EXECUTIVE. ZAKHEIM IS A MEMBER OF THE PROJECT FOR A NEW AMERICAN CENTURY AND WAS ALSO THE COMPTROLLER AT THE PENTAGON WHEN THE TRILLIONS OF DOLLARS WENT MISSING. OTHER IMPORTANT EVIDENCE SUGGESTS THAT THE TWIN TOWERS AND WORLD TRADE CENTER BUILDING 7 WERE BROUGHT DOWN VIA EXPLOSIVES IN A CONTROLLED DEMOLITION.

"I know many qualified engineers and scientists have said the WTC collapsed from explosives. In fact, if you look at the manner in which it fell, you have to give their conclusions credibility."

Paul Craig Roberts

AMONG THESE ARE EX-BRINGHAM YOUNG UNIVERSITY PHYSICS PROFESSOR DR. STEPHEN JONES, ENGINEER JEFF KING, MIT RESEARCHER JIM HOFFMAN, AND ARCHITECT RICHARD GAGE. THEY ARGUE THAT NEITHER THE IMPACT OF THE PLANES NOR THE BRIEFLY BURNING FIRES WHICH RESULTED CAN ACCOUNT FOR THE TOWERS' COLLAPSE. THEIR VIEWS ARE CORROBORATED BY NUMEROUS EYEWITNESS ACCOUNTS, INCLUDING THOSE OF FIREFIGHTERS IN THE TOWERS WHO REPORTED BOMBS GOING OFF, AND BY FOOTAGE OF THE EVENT WHICH SHOWS JETS OF DEBRIS BEING EJECTED FROM THE TOWERS MANY STORIES BELOW THE ACTUAL COLLAPSE. ANOTHER REMARKABLE DETAIL WHICH FEMA ACTUALLY ADMITS IN ITS REPORT IS WIDESPREAD CHEMICAL EVIDENCE CONSISTENT WITH THE INCENDIARY COMPOUND THERMATE THROUGHOUT THE REMAINS OF THE TOWERS.

FIRE CHIEF PALMER: "LADDER 15, WE'VE GOT TWO ISOLATED POCKETS OF FIRE. WE SHOULD BE ABLE TO KNOCK IT DOWN WITH TWO LINES."

TERESA VELIZ: "THERE WERE BOMBS GOING OFF EVERYWHERE. I WAS CONVINCED THERE WERE BOMBS PLANTED ALL OVER THE PLACE AND SOMEONE WAS SITTING AT A CONTROL PANEL PUSHING DETONATOR BUTTONS. THERE WAS ANOTHER EXPLOSION. AND ANOTHER. I DIDN'T KNOW WHICH WAY TO RUN."

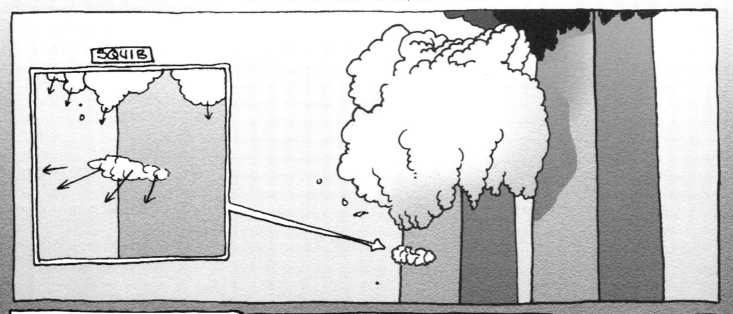

WORLD TRADE CENTER 7 WASN'T EVEN HIT BY A PLANE, NOR BY MAJOR DEBRIS FROM THE TWIN TOWERS. YET AROUND 5:20 THAT AFTERNOON, THIS 47-STORY STEEL-FRAMED BUILDING MYSTERIOUSLY IMPLODED SYMMETRICALLY INTO ITS OWN FOOTPRINT. LIKE THE TOWERS, IT WOULD BE TRULY REMARKABLE IF EVERY VERTICAL COLUMN IN THIS BUILDING HAD FAILED SIMULTANEOUSLY TO PRODUCE SUCH A NEAT COLLAPSE AT VIRTUAL FREE-FALL SPEED. MOST PEOPLE DON'T EVEN KNOW THAT WTC7 EVER EXISTED, THANKS TO THE WIDESPREAD MEDIA BLACKOUT ABOUT IT AFTER THE DAY OF THE ATTACKS.

CRITICS HAVE POINTED OUT THAT THE OFFICIAL REPORTS DESCRIBING THE COLLAPSE OF THE TOWERS VIOLATE THE SCIENTIFIC METHOD AT ALMOST EVERY TURN. AND WHAT WAS IN WTC7? IT HELD OFFICES FOR THE DoD, IRS, CIA, SECRET SERVICE, AND THOUSANDS OF SEC FILES ON ENRON AND OTHER CORPORATIONS UNDER INVESTIGATION. IT ALSO CONTAINED RUDY GIULLIANI'S SPECIALLY-REINFORCED COMMAND BUNKER, WHICH SOME HAVE SPECULATE WAS USED AS A COMMAND CENTER FOR THE WHOLE ATTACK.

BUT IF EXPLOSIVES WERE PLACED IN THE WORLD TRADE CENTER, WHO COULD HAVE DONE IT, AND WHEN? WOULD al-QAEDA OPERATIVES HAVE HAD THE REQUIRED ACCESS AND EXPERTISE? OR WAS IT SOMEONE FROM OUR OLD FRIEND, CONTROLLED DEMOLITION, INC., THE COMPANY WHICH ILLEGALLY DESTROYED THE EVIDENCE AFTER THE OKLAHOMA CITY BOMBING? THEY WERE CALLED IN AGAIN AFTER 9/11, BEFORE ANY REAL EXAMINATION OF THE WRECKAGE COULD TAKE PLACE. ALL OF THE BEAMS FROM THE WORLD TRADE CENTER WERE LOADED ONTO TRUCKS, SPECIALLY FITTED WITH THOUSAND-DOLLAR GPS LOCATOR DEVICES, THEN SHIPPED AT A DISCOUNT TO INDIA AND CHINA TO BE MELTED DOWN AS SCRAP.

THE CEO OF THE COMPANY IN CHARGE OF SECURITY FOR THE TOWERS (AND ALSO THE ELECTRONIC SECURITY SYSTEMS FOR UNITED AIRLINES) WAS THE PRESIDENT'S COUSIN, WIRT D. WALKER III,* AND MARVIN BUSH HAD ALSO SERVED THE COMPANY AS A PRINCIPAL. IN THE WEEKS LEADING UP TO 9/11, THERE WERE NUMEROUS UNUSUAL POWER-DOWNS AND EVACUATION DRILLS, AND THREE DAYS BEFORE THE ATTACKS, BOMB-SNIFFING DOGS WERE REMOVED FROM THE BUILDINGS.

*NOT HIMSELF A BONESMAN, BUT THERE HAVE BEEN 15 RELATED WALKERS IN THE ORDER

I wonder what all those engineers that keep coming in and out are up to?

THE IMPACT OF THE PLANES DIDN'T KILL VERY MANY PEOPLE. THE COLLAPSE KILLED THOUSANDS AND, ALONG WITH THE PSYCHOLOGICAL TRAUMA OF SEEING THE TWO LARGEST BUILDINGS ON NEW YORK'S SKYLINE DESTROYED BEFORE THEIR EYES, CONVINCED ENOUGH AMERICANS THAT THE BUSH ADMINISTRATION'S SUBSEQUENT ACTIONS WERE JUSTIFIED.

WHETHER ANY OF THESE SPECULATIONS ABOUT THE PHYSICAL DETAILS OF THE ATTACKS BEAR OUT OR NOT, THE OTHER EVIDENCE IS CLEAR. AND IT IS ALSO CLEAR WHO HAD THE MEANS, MOTIVE, AND OPPORTUNITY TO CARRY OUT THE ATTACKS, AND WHO TRIED TO STOP ANY INVESTIGATION. IF YOU STILL DOUBT THAT CRIMINAL ELEMENTS WITHIN OUR GOVERNMENT WOULD BE WILLING TO SACRIFICE THE LIVES OF NEARLY 3,000 AMERICAN CITIZENS ON 9/11 FOR FINANCIAL AND POLITICAL GAIN, CONSIDER WHAT THEY DID IMMEDIATELY AFTERWARDS.

Get A BRAIN! MORANS

GO USA

John Q

THE DESTRUCTION ON 9/11 RELEASED HUNDREDS OF TONS OF ASBESTOS AND LEAD POWDER INTO THE AIR, ENOUGH MERCURY TO CONTAMINATE 2,500 CITY BLOCKS, RADIOACTIVE AMERICIUM 241, AND A HOST OF OTHER CONTAMINANTS.

OVER HALF OF THE HEROIC GROUND ZERO RESCUE WORKERS NOW HAVE SERIOUS RESPIRATORY PROBLEMS, HUNDREDS OF FIREFIGHTERS CAN NO LONGER WORK, AND EVEN RESCUE DOGS HAVE DIED. THANKS TO THE FALSE ASSURANCES GIVEN TO NEW YORKERS, MORE PEOPLE MAY DIE FROM THE FALLOUT OF 9/11 THAN DIED IN THE ACTUAL ATTACKS.

"The alkalinity of the air was equivalent to that of DRANO. Yet starting on September 13th, the EPA maintained 'the air is safe to breathe.' A report by the EPA Inspector General in August of '03 revealed that EPA's press releases, which initially warned the public about asbestos in the air, were edited to offer reassurances instead. The editing was performed by the White House Council on Environmental Quality in order to reopen Wall Street. That's in the report."

Jenna Orkin

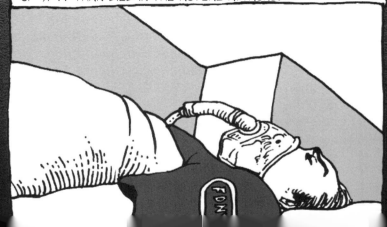

AND THOSE ANTHRAX ATTACKS THAT FOLLOWED 9/11? LUCKILY, PEOPLE IN THE WHITE HOUSE HAD THOUGHT TO GO ON THE ANTIBIOTIC CIPRO BEFORE THEY EVEN BEGAN. COINCIDENTALLY THE ANTHRAX WAS DISCOVERED TO BE AN ADVANCED STRAIN WHICH HAD ORIGINATED FROM FORT DETRICK IN FREDERICK, MARYLAND.

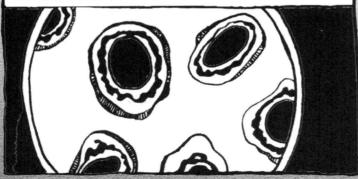

SO HOW HAS THE CABAL USED 9/11?

"There is a chance for the President of the United States to use this disaster to carry out what his father - a phrase his father used I think only once, and hasn't been used since - and that is a New World Order."

Gary Hart, US Commission on National Security 21st Century Co-Chair

THE U.S. INVADED AFGHANISTAN AND KICKED OUT THE TALIBAN, AFTER WHICH HEROIN PRODUCTION IN THE ''GOLDEN CRESCENT'' INCREASED TO SURPASS EVERY OTHER REGION IN THE WORLD.

THE U.S. INVADED IRAQ AND SECURED ACCESS TO OIL AND NATURAL GAS RESERVES WORTH ONE TRILLION DOLLARS.

DEFENSE CONTRACTORS LIKE THE CARLYLE GROUP (ANOTHER JOINT BUSH-BIN LADEN VENTURE) AND CONSTRUCTION COMPANIES LIKE HALLIBURTON (CHENEY'S PET) RECEIVED HUGE NO-BID CONTRACTS, WHILE BILLIONS WERE RUNG UP IN GOVERNMENT DEBT TO THE BANKS.

HALIBURTON

THE CARLYLE GROUP

FIGHTING FOR G.O.D. (Gold, Oil & Drugs)

The Neocons pushed through the USA-PATRIOT Act and the Military Commissions Act, shredding American civil liberties and massively building up the police state. Politicians are openly talking about using microchip implants to track, subliminally influence, or even shock people, and the media networks are promoting the idea.

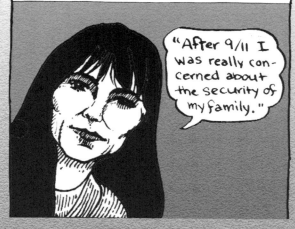

As Leslie Jacobs, the first person to volunteer for a microchip implant, confessed live on ABC:

"After 9/11 I was really concerned about the security of my family."

"I wouldn't mind having something planted permanently in my arm that would identify me."

Andy Rooney

"Those who would give up Essential Liberty for a little Temporary Safety deserve neither Liberty nor Safety."

Benjamin Franklin

Various presidential executive orders allow the president to declare martial law without congressional review for six months, and for the federal government to seize control of all modes of transportation, food sources, and to organize citizens into work brigades in labor camps.

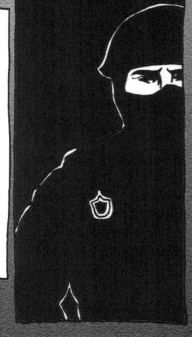

FEMA recently granted Halliburton $385 million to build concentration camps inside the United States.

The U.S. government has instituted an illegal program to spy on its own citizens, given the president authority to designate anyone as an enemy combatant, and dissolved habeas corpus, allowing secret military tribunals in place of impartial juries.

TALKS ARE ALREADY WELL UNDER WAY ABOUT A POSSIBLE NUCLEAR STRIKE ON IRAN, AND THERE HAVE BEEN REPORTS OF COVERT U.S. ACTIONS WITHIN THAT COUNTRY.

Iran

BUT THE REAL GEM, THE ULTIMATE GOAL, IS THE NUMBER-ONE ITEM ON THE PENTAGON'S WISH LIST: A TRILLION DOLLAR ORBITAL MISSILE PLATFORM, WHICH, IT IS OPENLY STATED, WOULD BE USED TO QUELL RESISTANCE, ANYWHERE IN THE WORLD, RESULTING FROM THE INCREASING DISPARITY BETWEEN THE HAVES AND HAVE-NOTS. THERE HAS BEEN AT LEAST ONE ARMED SATELLITE IN ORBIT SINCE 2004 (N-FIRE), AND IN OCTOBER 2006, BUSH AUTHORIZED THE GO-AHEAD FOR A MASSIVE BUILD-UP OF WEAPONS IN SPACE.

"This war on terror is bogus: The 9/11 attacks gave the US an ideal pretext to use force to secure its global domination."

Michael Meacher, British MP, former Environmental Minister.

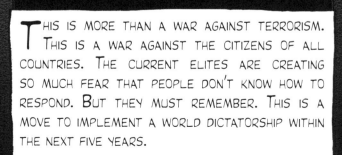

THIS IS MORE THAN A WAR AGAINST TERRORISM. THIS IS A WAR AGAINST THE CITIZENS OF ALL COUNTRIES. THE CURRENT ELITES ARE CREATING SO MUCH FEAR THAT PEOPLE DON'T KNOW HOW TO RESPOND. BUT THEY MUST REMEMBER. THIS IS A MOVE TO IMPLEMENT A WORLD DICTATORSHIP WITHIN THE NEXT FIVE YEARS.

—DR. JOHANNES KOEPPL, A FORMER GERMAN DEFENSE MINISTRY OFFICIAL AND NATO ADVISOR

So what can we do about all of this? First, educate ourselves.

Second, educate our friends and families.

We can talk with one another. Discuss the future we envision.

Learn to see past our differences. This is bigger than Left and Right, Black and White.

THE MORE THAT US COMMON PEOPLE EXPRESS OUR VIEWS, THE MORE FAMOUS PEOPLE WILL TAKE THE RISK OF SPEAKING OUT, DRAWING EVEN MORE REGULAR FOLKS INTO THE FOLD. JUST LOOK AT ALL THE MAINSTREAM MUSIC AND MOVIES THAT HAVE COME OUT RECENTLY DEPICTING THE EVILS OF THE NEW WORLD ORDER...

Only together can we win, and we have to beat the established system as a whole. What may have started as a conspiracy between a few people centuries ago has grown into a self-perpetuating machine, where someone will always be ready to step in for any individual who is removed.

With its tanks and nuclear weapons and secret police, the "New World Order" can seem terrifying and invincible. But its power is largely dependent on an illusion, and people believing that illusion. We are poised at a unique moment in history. Will we sit back in apathy and allow others to decide our fate, or will we choose lives which are intense and full in the struggle for our freedom and our very existence?

"If you love wealth more than liberty, the tranquility of servitude better than the animating contest of freedom, depart from us in peace. We ask not your council nor your arms. Crouch down and lick the hand that feeds you. May your chains rest lightly upon you and may posterity forget that you were our countrymen."

Samuel Adams

WHAT ELSE CAN WE DO?

SUPPORT CAMPAIGN FINANCE REFORM. UNTIL POLITICAL CAMPAIGNS ARE PUBLICLY FINANCED, ONLY THE WEALTHY AND WELL-CONNECTED HAVE MUCH OF A CHANCE AT GETTING INTO OFFICE.

SUPPORT MEDIA REFORM. DEMOCRACY REQUIRES AN INFORMED CITIZENRY, WHICH IS NOT POSSIBLE WHEN MOST OF OUR NEWS IS MEDIATED BY A HANDFUL OF MEGA-CORPORATIONS.

SUPPORT INSTANT RUN-OFF VOTING. UNDER THIS SYSTEM, YOU DON'T HAVE TO VOTE FOR THE LESSER OF TWO EVILS. YOU WOULD BE ALLOWED TO MAKE TWO OR MORE CHOICES IN A GIVEN RACE, RANKING THE CANDIDATES. IF YOUR FIRST CHOICE (PERHAPS A DARK HORSE OR THIRD PARTY CANDIDATE) DIDN'T GET ENOUGH VOTES, THEN YOUR VOTE WOULD COUNT TOWARDS YOUR NEXT CHOICE.

ONLY VOTE FOR CANDIDATES WHO SIGN AN AFFIDAVIT SWEARING TO WORK TO ABOLISH THE FEDERAL RESERVE.

HOLD YOUR ALREADY ELECTED OFFICIALS ACCOUNTABLE. CALL, WRITE, AND FAX YOUR REPRESENTATIVES REGULARLY TO DEMAND A NEW INVESTIGATION INTO 9/11.

VOTE WITH YOUR DOLLAR. INSTEAD OF KEEPING YOUR SAVINGS AT SOME MEGA-BANK, CONSIDER A LOCAL CREDIT UNION. INSTEAD OF SHOPPING ON THE INTERNET OR CHAIN RETAILERS, SUPPORT YOUR LOCAL ECONOMY. INSTEAD OF GOING TO THE BIG SUPERMARKET, BUY FOOD FROM A LOCAL FARMERS' MARKET.

RELY ON YOURSELF AND YOUR COMMUNITY INSTEAD OF THE GOVERNMENT AND BIG CORPORATIONS. GET TO KNOW YOUR NEIGHBORS. OWN FIREARMS AND KNOW HOW TO USE THEM. SUPPORT A COMMUNITY GARDEN, OR START A GARDEN OF YOUR OWN. IF YOU WORK A WHITE COLLAR JOB BE SURE YOU KNOW SOME BLUE COLLAR SKILLS. IF YOU WORK A BLUE COLLAR JOB, BE SURE YOU KNOW HOW TO USE COMPUTERS, BECAUSE THEY ARE PERHAPS THE MOST POWERFUL TOOLS AN INDIVIDUAL CAN OWN.

EDUCATE THE PUBLIC. COPY FLIERS AND DVDs AND PASS THEM OUT TO FRIENDS AND STRANGERS. HANG BANNERS AND POSTERS OVER HIGHWAYS. PUT UP STICKERS AND STENCILS. SPEAK AT OPEN MICS. POST ON INTERNET FORUMS. UTILIZE SOCIAL NETWORKING SITES LIKE MYSPACE OR CREATE YOUR OWN WEBSITE. HOST A REGULAR 9/11 MOVIE NIGHT. ORGANIZE AND/OR ATTEND PROTEST RALLIES (ESPECIALLY ON 11TH OF EVERY MONTH, WHICH IS ALREADY AN ONGOING NATIONAL CAMPAIGN). JOIN A LOCAL 9/11 TRUTH GROUP OR START YOUR OWN AND GET OTHERS INVOLVED!

NOTES & FURTHER READING

PAGE 40

PNAC DOCUMENTS

VISIT THEIR OWN WEBSITE:
<WWW.NEWAMERICANCENTURY.ORG>

KEN WILLIAMS WARNINGS

CNN.COM 5/21/02, "SENATORS QUESTION 'PHOENIX MEMO' AUTHOR"; CBS NEWS 5/15/02, "FLIGHT SCHOOL MEMO NAMED BIN LADEN"

COLEEN ROWLEY

TIME 5/21/02, "COLEEN ROWLEY'S MEMO TO FBI DIRECTOR ROBERT MUELLER"; USA TODAY 5/28/02 "LETTER SHIFTS HEAT TO FBI"

SIBEL EDMONDS

INDEPENDENT 4/02/04, "'I SAW PAPERS THAT SHOW U.S. KNEW AL-QA'IDA WOULD ATTACK CITIES WITH AEROPLANES'; WHISTLE-BLOWER THE WHITE HOUSE WANTS TO SILENCE SPEAKS TO THE INDEPENDENT"

ISRAEL'S WARNING

TELEGRAPH 9/15/01, "ISRAELI SECURITY ISSUED URGENT WARNING TO CIA OF LARGE-SCALE TERROR ATTACKS"

TALIBAN'S WARNING

BBC NEWS WORLD EDITION 9/7/02, "TALEBAN 'WARNED U.S. OF HUGE ATTACK'"

PAGE 41

"NO WARNINGS"

OFFICE OF THE WHITE HOUSE PRESS SECRETARY 9/11/01

ASHCROFT STOPS FLYING COMMERCIAL FLIGHTS

CBS NEWS 7/26/01, "ASHCROFT FLYING HIGH"

WILLIE BROWN'S WARNING

SF CHRONICLE 9/12/01, "WILLIE BROWN GOT LOW-KEY EARLY WARNING ABOUT AIR TRAVEL"

PENTAGON OFFICIALS CANCEL FLIGHTS

NEWSWEEK 9/24/01, "BUSH: 'WE'RE AT WAR'"

SILVERSTEIN'S DOCTOR'S APPOINTMENT

NY MAGAZINE 4/18/05, "WHO WANTS TO MOVE TO GROUND ZERO?"

BUSH'S COUSIN SAVED

ANANOVA 9/18/01, "PRESIDENT'S COUSIN

PAGE 42

PUT OPTIONS

AP 9/18/01, "EXCHANGE EXAMINES ODD JUMP BEFORE ATTACK: MANY PUT OPTIONS OF HIJACKED PLANES' PARENT COMPANIES PURCHASED"; SF CHRONICLE 9/19/01, "NEW SCRUTINY OF AIRLINES OPTIONS DEALS"; INDEPENDENT 10/14/01, "MYSTERY OF TERROR 'INSIDER DEALERS'"

RIGGS BANK

WASHINGTON POST 1/28/05, "RIGGS BANK AGREES TO GUILTY PLEA AND FINE"; NY TIMES 5/14/04, "REGULATORS FINE RIGGS $25 MILLION"; CNN 5/13/04, "BANK FINED $25 MILLION IN TERRORISM PROBE"

PAGE 43

OSAMA'S HOSPITAL STAY

GUARDIAN 11/01/01, "CIA AGENT ALLEGED TO HAVE MET BIN LADEN IN JULY"; CBS 1/28/02, "HOSPITAL WORKER: I SAW OSAMA"

SPECIAL FORCES MURDER/SUICIDES

INDEPENDENT 8/2/02; CNN 7/27/02, "FORT BRAGG KILLINGS RAISE ALARM ABOUT STRESS"

UNMASKING THE DECEPTION
by Carol Broulliet

Almost everyone can remember with clarity the moment that they heard of the attacks of September 11th, and in addition to the grief, shock, horror, fear that we felt was the desire to understand, to know. Why? How? Who could possibly benefit from such a crime? These questions were never answered satisfactorily by the press, which soon began beating the war drums and hurtling us towards World War III.

The U.S. government's attacks upon Afghanistan, the Bill of Rights, the Constitution, and Iraq, its attempt to redefine the world in an Orwellian manner contingent upon the events of September 11th, prompted people to critically examine the events of that day, before, and after in order to discern the truth from the spin.

Concerned people sought to build a new map of reality, to understand where we were, and what direction we were suddenly facing. Confusion and disorientation make it difficult to know which way to go: with a good map, a sense of where we have been and where we are heading, people are empowered to change course, and not blindly follow "a leader." The worldwide Web facilitated collaborations through an extraordinary exchange of information and observations in an urgent, spontaneous effort to make sense of what happened. Use of the Web helped to put together the pieces of a puzzle, and see the big picture of the crisis as it unfolded. Yet the carefully cordoned "reality" defined by the mainstream press remained unquestioned by many.

In 2002, 10,000 Deception Dollars were printed and given away at a San Francisco anti-war march; people loved them. Since then, over six million more — including Media Deception and Election Deception Dollars — have been distributed. Our most popular leaflet/consciousness raiser on 9-11, the Deception Dollars help us to reach directly to people who have been bombarded with mainstream and government propaganda and who want to know the truth. We firmly

NOTES & FURTHER READING

PAGE 44
MIRACULOUS ESCAPE FROM AFGHANISTAN
PBS *FRONTLINE* 6/20/06; *KNIGHT RIDDER* 10/20/02, "TORA BORA A LOST VICTORY U.S. PASSED UP OPPORTUNITIES TO QUASH AL-QAIDA"; *LONDON TIMES* 7/22/02, "HOW BIN LADEN'S HUGE CONVOY GAVE AMERICAN FORCES THE SLIP"; *CHRISTIAN SCIENCE MONITOR* 3/4/02, "HOW BIN LADEN GOT AWAY"; *USA TODAY* 1/2/02, "U.S. REQUEST LET BIN LADEN ESCAPE SAYS TOP AFGHAN COMMANDER"

AIRLIFT OF EVIL
NEW YORKER 1/21/02, "THE GETAWAY"; *NOW WITH BILL MOYERS* 2/21/03

PAGE 44
BIN LADEN "CONFESSION TAPE"
CNN 12/14/01; *USA TODAY* 12/13/01, "VIDEO TAPE SIMPLY CONFIRMS VIEWS"

MUSLIMS GONE WILD
SF CHRONICLE 10/4/01, "AGENTS OF TERROR LEAVE THEIR MARK ON SIN CITY"; *WALL STREET JOURNAL* 10/10/01, "TERRORIST STAG PARTY"; *LA TIMES* 9/1/02, "THE PLOT"; *USA TODAY* 9/14/01, "MANAGER: MAN SPEWED ANTI-AMERICAN

SENTIMENTS"; DANIEL HOPSICKER, *WELCOME TO TERRORLAND* (MADCOW PRESS, 2004)

FABRICATED EVIDENCE
CNN 9/17/01, 9/11 COMMISSION; *SYDNEY MORNING HERALD* 9/15/01, "ONE-WAY TICKETS TO HELL"

PAGE 46
GAMBLING ON ABRAMOFF'S SHIP
ST. PETERSBURG TIMES 9/27/01, "HIJACKERS LINKED TO LOCAL CRUISE"; *USA TODAY* 9/27/01, "JUSTICE DEPT. RELEASES PHOTOS OF SUSPECTED HIJACKERS"

GOSS & AHMED
WASHINGTON POST 5/18/02, "A CLOAK BUT NO DAGGER"

*INTERESTINGLY, RELATIONS BETWEEN PAKISTAN AND THE U.S. HAVE SOURED RECENTLY. IN LATE 2006 PAKISTANI DICTATOR GENERAL MUSHARRAF OUTED OMAR SHEIKH AS AN MI-6 AGENT. <HTTP://WWW.THENEWS.COM.PK/TOP _ STORY _ DETAIL.ASP?ID=3313>

PAGE 47
MISSING TRILLIONS
CBS 9/10/01; CBS 1/29/02, "THE WAR ON WASTE"; *SF CHRONICLE* 5/18/03,

"MILITARY WASTE UNDER FIRE"

NORAD CRASH SIMULATIONS
USA TODAY 4/18/04, "NORAD HAS DRILLS OF JETS AS WEAPONS"; *BOSTON GLOBE* 4/14/04, "PENTAGON CRASH 'TOO UNREALISTIC'"

CONDI
CBS 5/17/02

PAGE 47
WAR GAMES
HTTP://WWW.GLOBALSECURITY.ORG/MILITARY/OPS/AMALGAM-VIRGO.HTM; AMERICAN FORCES INFORMATION SERVICE 2/20/07; C-SPAN 2/11/05

PAGE 49
WTC7
JOURNAL OF 9/11 STUDIES 9/06, "WHY INDEED DID THE WTC BUILDINGS COMPLETELY COLLAPSE?"

NY TIMES 2/19/89, "COMMERCIAL PROPERTY: THE SALOMON SOLUTION; A BUILDING WITHIN A BUILDING, AT A COST OF $200 MILLION"

*FURTHERMORE, THESE BUILDINGS WERE ALL INCREDIBLY STRONG. AS SILVERSTEIN SAID OF

believe that the truth will bring together the majority of the world's people who seek peace, justice, a better world for their children and all life. They will see through the lies of a tiny global minority clinging to power through deception, war, terrorism and fear. We invite everyone to join our efforts to learn and expose the truth about 9-11, a crime which is being

used to justify a war of terrorism against all of us. We hope to nurture a spirit of cooperation, respect, love amongst all who realize how interdependent our future is.

A Global Dance has begun between the forces of Peace and War, Truth and Lies, Resistance and Repression. An elite minority who control the resources of the U.S. government, and transnational corporations benefit from war, and will do what they can to create fear and confusion in order to maintain

their power. All we can do is tell the truth, shatter the BIG LIE, with facts, humor, love, courage, creativity, and clarity, empowering all of us to hold accountable those responsible for crimes against humanity, and to rein them in before they commit worse acts of terror against people at home and abroad.

The Deception Dollars were created as a portal to the best information we have found on 9-11. There is so much information that no one could possibly keep up with it all, and there is a tremendous diversity of ideas, opinions, observations amongst a growing number of sites. Research on each site provides links to other sites. Some sites provide a place for dialogue, discussion, organizing opportunities. Some just try to convey essential information. There are more URLs for 9-11 sites than space on the Deception Dollars to list them, but — hopefully — the breadth, diversity and widespread nature of the internet will help to grow an unstoppable movement.

You can help, and only you can decide how and where your talents, skills, energy can be best deployed to further the cause of truth, peace, justice, life.

WWW.DECEPTIONDOLLAR.COM

NOTES & FURTHER READING

WTC7, "WE BUILT IN ENOUGH REDUNDANCY TO ALLOW ENTIRE PORTIONS OF FLOORS TO BE REMOVED WITHOUT AFFECTING THE BUILDING'S STRUCTURAL INTEGRITY, ON THE ASSUMPTION THAT SOMEONE MIGHT NEED DOUBLE-HEIGHT FLOORS."

PAGE 50
DESTRUCTION OF EVIDENCE
USA TODAY 3/6/02, "CONGRESSIONAL PANEL FOCUSES ON WHY WTC COLLAPSED"; HINA.ORG.CN 1/24/02, "BAOSTEEL WILL RECYCLE WORLD TRADE CENTER DEBRIS"

GPS LOCATER DEVICES
ACCESS CONTROL & SECURITY SYSTEMS (SECURITYSOLUTIONS.COM) 6/1/02, "GPS ON THE JOB IN MASSIVE WORLD TRADE CENTER CLEAN-UP"

CONTROLLED DEMOLITION, INC
WASTE AGE 10/16/01, "CONSTRUCTION COMPANY PROPOSES PLAN FOR WTC SITE"

PAGE 52
BOMB DOGS REMOVED
NEWSDAY 9/12/01

TOXIC DUST
COUNTERPUNCH 5/13/05, "EPA'S NEW MONITORING PLAN STILL INADEQUATE GROUND ZERO'S TOXIC DUST"; VILLAGE VOICE 11/28/06, "DEATH BY DUST"

PAGE 53
CIPRO
WASHINGTON POST 10/23/01, "WHITE HOUSE MAIL MACHINE HAS ANTHRAX"

OPIUM PRODUCTION SKYROCKETS AFTER AMERICAN INVASION
OBSERVER 11/25/01, "VICTORIOUS WARLORDS SET TO OPEN OPIUM FLOODGATES"; INDEPENDENT 11/21/01, "OPIUM FARMERS REJOICE AT THE DEFEAT OF THE TALIBAN"; INDEPENDENT 9/26/02, "MASSIVE POSTWAR RISE IN PRODUCTION OF AFGHAN OPIUM"

PAGE 54
LESLIE JACOBS
WIRED NEWS 2/6/02, "THEY WANT THEIR ID CHIPS NOW"

WHEN I DESPAIR, I REMEMBER THAT ALL THROUGH HISTORY THE WAY OF TRUTH AND LOVE HAS ALWAYS WON. THERE HAVE BEEN TYRANTS AND MURDERERS AND FOR A TIME THEY SEEM INVINCIBLE BUT IN THE END, THEY ALWAYS FALL — THINK OF IT, ALWAYS.

—MOHANDAS K. GANDHI

FIGHTING FOR G.O.D. (GOLD, OIL & DRUGS)

9/11 ORGANIZATIONS & WEB SITES

CENTER FOR COOPERATIVE RESEARCH

Projects include Complete 911 Timeline, Inquiry into the Invasion of Iraq, and History of U.S. Interventions. www.cooperativeresearch.org

9/11 CITIZENSWATCH

Citizen-led oversight process established to monitor and constructively engage the government-sanctioned National Commission on the Terrorist Attacks on the United States. www.911citizenswatch.org

9/11 DECEPTION DOLLAR

Deception Dollars help to reach directly to people who have been bombarded with mainstream and government propaganda. www.deceptiondollar.com

911TRUTH.ORG

Campaign to educate the public about the September 11th cover-up and expose the truth surrounding the events of 9/11. www.911truth.org

PEACEFUL TOMORROWS

Advocacy group founded by family members of September 11th victims. Seeks effective nonviolent responses. www.peacefultomorrows.org

communitycurrency.org	911research.wtc7.net
complete911timeline.org	911review.com
crisisinamerica.org	oilempire.us
fromthewilderness.com	ratical.org
globalresearch.ca	rigorousintuition.ca
indymedia.org	space4peace.org
madcowpress.com	truthaction.org
911blogger.com	truthmove.org

911independentcommission.org

9/11 BOOKS

THE BIG WEDDING BY SANDER HICKS
CROSSING THE RUBICON BY MICHAEL RUPPERT
THE NEW PEARL HARBOR BY DAVID RAY GRIFFIN
OMISSIONS AND DISTORTIONS BY DAVID RAY GRIFFIN
THE TERROR TIMELINE BY PAUL THOMPSON
TOWERS OF DECEPTION BY BARRIE ZWICKER
THE WAR ON TRUTH BY NAFEEZ AHMED
WELCOME TO TERRORLAND BY DANIEL HOPSICKER
WAKING UP FROM OUR NIGHTMARE BY DON PAUL AND JIM HOFFMAN
AMERICA'S WAR ON TERRORISM... BY MICHEL CHOSSUDOVSKY

9/11 & ANTI-FASCISM DVDs

AFTERMATH - UNANSWERED QUESTIONS FROM 9/11

With the increasing controversy surrounding the federal probe into the September 11 terrorist attacks, Guerilla News Network (GNN) decided to pre-empt the government and produce its own version of a "truth commission."

AMERICA: FREEDOM TO FASCISM

This film shows in great detail and with undeniable facts that America is moving headlong toward a fascist police state. Wake up!

CLEAR THE SKIES - 9/11 AIR DEFENSE

The trategic response to the terrorist attacks of September 11, 2001 is thoroughly analyzed in the riveting BBC documentary.

THE CORPORATION

This documentary is transforming audiences with its insightful and compelling analysis. Taking its status as a legal "person" to the logical conclusion, the film puts the corporation on the psychiatrist's couch to ask, "What kind of person is it?"

EVERYBODY'S GOTTA LEARN SOMETIME

Largely ignored by the mainstream media, many of the disturbing facts surrounding the attacks of 9/11 raise deeply ethical questions associated with issues of accountability, justice and censorship in America.

THE FOURTH WORLD WAR

From the front-lines of conflicts in Mexico, Argentina, South Africa, Palestine, Korea, Seattle and Genoa, to the 'War on Terror' in New York, Afghanistan, and Iraq, this is a story of men and women around the world who resist being annihilated in this war.

IMPROBABLE COLLAPSE: THE DEMOLITION OF OUR REPUBLIC

A film that looks at the events of September 11, 2001 from a scientific perspective.

MARTIAL LAW 911: THE RISE OF THE POLICE STATE

Filmed primarily during the Republican Party's 2004 national convention in New York, the film shows signs of a growing police state.

MOHAMED ATTA & THE VENICE FLYING CIRCUS

Three of the four terrorist pilots learned to fly in tiny Venice, Florida, a sleepy retirement community. Why?

9/11 & AMERICAN EMPIRE: INTELLECTUALS SPEAK OUT

Presentations by David Ray Griffin, Peter Dale Scott, Peter Phillips and Kevin Ryan.

9/11 CITIZENS COMMISSION

Excellent as an introduction to the best evidence of complicity. Speakers include Cynthia McKinney, Michael Ruppert, Barrie Zwicker, John Judge, Michael Springman, Indira Singh, and others.

9/11 PRESS FOR TRUTH

"We felt the country was at risk from terrorists and from incompetence... and maybe worse." —Lorie Van Auken, September 11th Widow

THE OIL FACTOR: BEHIND THE WAR ON TERROR

Questioning the motives for the U.S. wars in the Middle-East and Central Asia, where 3/4 of the world's oil and natural gas is located.

OKC BOMBING - FORERUNNER TO 9/11

According to the federal theory, the bombing in Oklahoma City, at the Alfred P. Murrah Building on April 19, 1995, was the work of American dissidents bent on a violent overthrow of the government.

SECRET HEARTBEAT OF AMERICA

An two-hour long examination of the CIA, the Drug Trade and its impact.

TERRORSTORM

Surveying the depths of history from the Gulf of Tonkin through to the Madrid and 7/7 London bombings, this film robustly catalogues the real story.

THE TRUTH & LIES OF 9/11

Portland State University Lecture by Mike Ruppert.

WACO: THE RULES OF ENGAGEMENT

An incredibly powerful examination of the events that led up to the fire at the Davidian Branch compound that took the lives of seventy men, women and children.

WHO KILLED JOHN O'NEIL?

Traumatized by the September 11th attacks, one man struggles to dismantle official history, at the expense of his sanity and even his life. Grappling with multiple realities - and multiple personalities - he must retreat into his mind in pursuit of the truth. In a fictional film about non-fictional events, there is a place where belief and faith will blind you, where nothing is sacred, and to get there all you have to do is ask "Who killed John O'Neil?"

TRINEDAY'S FEATURED TITLES

The True Story of the Bilderberg Group
BY DANIEL ESTULIN

More than a center of influence, the Bilderbergers are a shadow world government deciding in total secrecy at annual meetings their plans of domination.

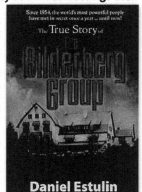

The True Story of the Bilderberg Group goes inside the secret meetings and sheds light on why a group of politicians, businessmen, bankers and mighty individuals formed the world's most powerful society. It was Benjamin Disraeli, England's Prime Minister, who noted that "The world is governed by very different personages from what is imagined by those who are not behind the scenes."

The True Story of the Bilderberg Group includes unpublished and never-before-seen photographs and documents of meetings, as it exposes the past, present and future plans of the Bilderberg elite.

Softcover: **$24.95** (ISBN: 0977795349) • 350 pages • Size: 6 x 9
—Available September 2007—

Rigorous Intuition
What You Don't Know Can't Hurt Them
BY JEFF WELLS

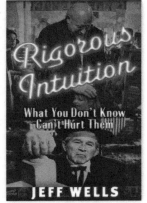

Distinguished by setting both intellectual rigor and mature intuition to the difficult subjects that define our time and yet frequently receive neither, *Rigorous Intuition* is a welcome source of analysis and commentary for those prepared to go deeper, and darker, than even most alternative media permit. From 9/11 to elite pedophile rings to "High Weirdness" and beyond, Wells separates the signal from the noise, and makes the connections that both describe our alarming predicament and suggest a strategy for taking back our world. "What you don't know can't hurt them" – so goes the maxim of *Rigorous Intuition*. "In Jeff's hands, tinfoil hats become crowns and helmets of the purest gold." —Ellen Guldi

Softcover **$19.95**
(ISBN 0977795322) • 256 PAGES • Size: 5.5 x 8.5
—Available 2007—

Jaded Tasks
Brass Plates. Black Ops, & Big Oil — The Blood Politics of George Bush & Co.
BY WAYNE MADSEN

This investigative account details how America's economic and intelligence associations with Saudi Arabia and Pakistan led to the devastating September 11 attacks and illustrates the role that private military companies are playing in George W. Bush's "new world order." Based on personal interviews, never-before-published classified documents, and extensive research, this examination details the criminal forces thought to rule the world today—the Bush cartel, Russian-Ukranian-Israeli mafia, and Wahhabist Saudi terror financiers—revealing links between these groups and disastrous events such as 9/11.

Wayne scares the hell out of the Military-Industrial-Mendacity Complex — Greg Palast
Paperback: **$19.95**, 320 Pages, 5.5 x 8.5

Dr. Mary's Monkey
How the Unsolved Murder of a Doctor, a Secret Laboratory in New Orleans and Cancer-Causing Monkey Viruses are Linked to Lee Harvey Oswald, the JFK Assassination and Emerging Global Epidemics
BY EDWARD T. HASLAM, FOREWORD BY JIM MARRS
Evidence of top-secret medical experiments and cover-ups of clinical blunders

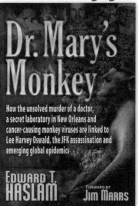

The 1964 murder of a nationally known cancer researcher sets the stage for this gripping exposé of medical professionals enmeshed in covert government operations over the course of three decades. Following a trail of police records, FBI files, cancer statistics, and medical journals, this revealing book presents evidence of a web of medical secret-keeping that began with the handling of evidence in the JFK assassination and continued apace, sweeping doctors into cover-ups of cancer outbreaks, contaminated polio vaccine, the genesis of the AIDS virus, and biological weapon research using infected monkeys.

Softcover: **$19.95** (ISBN: 0977795306) • 320 pages • Size: 5 1/2 x 8 1/2

The Franklin Scandal
A Story of Powerbrokers, Child Abuse & Betrayal
BY NICK BRYANT

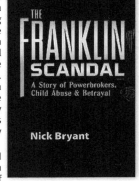

A chilling exposé of corporate corruption and government cover-ups, this account of a nationwide child-trafficking and pedophilia ring tells a sordid tale of corruption in high places. The scandal originally surfaced during an investigation into Omaha, Nebraska's failed Franklin Federal Credit Union and took the author beyond the Midwest and ultimately to Washington, DC. Implicating businessmen, senators, major media corporations, the CIA, and even the venerable Boys Town organization, this extensively researched report includes firsthand interviews with key witnesses and explores a controversy that has received scant media attention.

The Franklin Scandal is the story of a underground ring that pandered children to a cabal of the rich and powerful. The ring's pimps were a pair of Republican powerbrokers who used Boys Town as a pedophiliac reservoir, and had access to the highest levels of our government and connections to the CIA.

Hardcover: **$24.95** (ISBN: 0977795357) • 350 pages • Size: 6 x 9
—Available January 2008—

Fixing America
Breaking the Strangehold of Corporate Rule, Big Media, and the Religious Right
BY JOHN BUCHANAN, FOREWORD BY JOHN MCCONNELL
An explosive analysis of what ails the United States

An award-winning investigative reporter provides a clear, honest diagnosis of corporate rule, big media, and the religious right in this damning analysis. Exposing the darker side of capitalism, this critique raises alarms about the security of democracy in today's society, including the rise of the corporate state, the insidious role of professional lobbyists, the emergence of religion and theocracy as a right-wing political tactic, the failure of the mass media, and the sinister presence of an Orwellian neo-fascism.

Softcover: **$19.95**, (ISBN 0-975290681) 216 Pages, 5.5 x 8.5

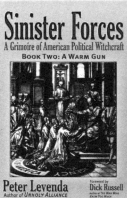

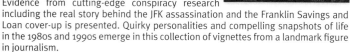